Security for the Householder
Fitting Locks and other Devices

Security for the Householder
Fitting Locks and other Devices

E. Phillips LCGI

Guild of Master Craftsman Publications Ltd

First published 1997 by
Guild of Master Craftsman Publications Ltd
166 High Street, Lewes
East Sussex BN7 1XU

© Eddie Phillips 1997

Photographs by Eddie Phillips (except those listed below)

Photographs on pages 17 (Fig 2.5), 20 (Fig 2.12), 26, (Fig 2.26), 46 (Fig 3.11), 102 (Fig 11.2), and 103 (Figs 11.3, 11.4, 11.5) by Anthony Bailey

Drawings by Tim Benké

Cover photograph by Anthony Bailey

ISBN 1 86108 060 3

Designed by Fineline Studios

Set in Frutiger

Colour separation by Viscan Graphics, Singapore

Printed in Hong Kong by H & Y Printing Ltd

I dedicate this book to my wife Margaret who proved to be an endless source of encouragement to me and a valuable proofreader

ACKNOWLEDGEMENTS

I would like to thank the following people for their assistance in compiling the information for the book: Allister Boyd, Manager of R Bernard Ironmongers in Birkenhead, for allowing me to set up in the store and photograph a range of items shown in the book; David Hoggan, Senior Brand Manager for Polycell Products Ltd, for his generous assistance in sending me a range of locks to use and photograph; B & Q Warehouse in Wallasey for allowing me to photograph security grill units sold within the store; finally all the staff at GMC Publications for their hard work.

Contents

Introduction

Whether you have only recently moved in or have been resident for many years in the same house, your home and its contents are always vulnerable to burglary, and many people do not realize how inadequate their security measures against break-ins actually are. Standard cylinder locks without a deadlocking facility are notoriously easy to open, sometimes only requiring that a credit card be slid down between the lock and the door frame. The windows of many homes are only secured by their lever handles, or, in the case of sash windows, their window stays, and offer easy access to the experienced burglar.

Additional security locks are not hard to fit, provide increased protection, and often act as a deterrent, preventing wilful damage to the property; if a would-be intruder realizes a door or window is firmly secured, he is less likely to even attempt to break in because of the amount of time this would take and the noise such a process may generate.

This book is designed to provide you with advice on all manner of security-related matters, and to act as an easy-to-use reference manual, allowing you to quickly find the information you need. Chapter 1 shows you how to assess your home and outbuildings in order to decide the type and number of extra security measures you can take. This will also help you assess the cost, and prioritize your needs if necessary.

The remaining chapters show you how to secure windows and doors around your home. The more labour-intensive security devices such as mortise locks (commonly known as 'Chubb' locks after the manufacturer) are given chapters of their own so that the instructions are as comprehensive as possible. The book is fully cross-referenced throughout, so you should have no trouble in looking up what you need to know.

Chapters 2 and 3 give details on the *construction* of various common types of window and door, as well as suggesting ways to make them more secure. I strongly recommend you read these chapters, as well as Chapter 1, no matter what your needs may be, as you will find this basic knowledge extremely useful when it comes to understanding some of the terminology used later in the book. For quick reference there is also a glossary of terms, on pages 105–6, a list of tools you will need, on page 107, and a comprehensive index on pages 111–13.

Assessing
the needs
of your home

B egin by looking at the outside of your property in order to identify the areas most likely to be used to gain access. You will need to draw up a list of security fittings that will reduce the risk of forced entry, and once you have a full list of projects to tackle, you should prioritize the most vulnerable areas and secure those first.

As a general rule, the ground floor windows and doors are considered to be more vulnerable than the upper floors, but if you have an attached garage with a window above it, a large tree close to the house, trellis work strong enough to hold a person's weight or any other means of easily gaining access to the upper levels, then these areas must also be regarded as prime targets. Don't forget to examine any outbuildings you may have, as you may wish to secure these as well; sheds and garages are a prime target for thieves.

Compile a list of all the doors, windows and gates you feel need attention. Don't worry about what type of fittings to use at this stage as this will become apparent as you read on through the book. Just list all vulnerable areas of access to give yourself an idea of the type and amount of work involved.

Assessing windows

Ask yourself the following questions:

▼ What are the windows made of – wood, metal or UPVC (plastic)?

▼ How many *opening* windows are there? Include all openings however small, and do not omit those that *should* open but are stuck fast with paint!

▼ How many 'fixed lights' (i.e. windows with no opening sash) are there?

▼ How many windows are top hung (i.e. hinged at the top)?

▼ How many windows are side hung (i.e. hinged at the side)?

▼ Do any windows hinge in the middle, and pivot to open?

▼ Are any of the opening sections of the windows of the louvre slat type? These are particularly vulnerable and should be secured or replaced. If you can't afford to replace a louvre window, a suggestion is given on page 36 in Chapter 2 for how to temporarily upgrade louvre slats until a replacement window can be fitted.

As you give consideration to the security of the windows please keep in mind the need to provide a means of escape in an emergency if you mislay the key (see Fig 2.25 on page 26).

Once you have documented all the window details, turn your attention to the external doors.

Assessing external doors

How many hinges are fitted? I recommend that three sets (or 1½ pairs) be fitted to external doors, as such doors are heavier than internal doors. You will find full instructions on how to fit a third hinge on page 51.

Open each door and see if the existing hinges have interlocking security lugs (see Fig 1.1). If not, you should look at the possibility of changing them for a more secure hinge, and this is covered on page 50 in Chapter 4.

Now check to see how soundly the door is constructed. Look at the top, middle and bottom rail joints (see Fig 1.2) to check for joint movement or timber decay, as this dramatically reduces the security of a door. Chapter 3 (see page 37) provides guidance on door construction and the types of fittings needed to provide adequate security. Chapters 5–11 provide detailed information on how to fit specific locks, bolts and other devices.

You should also give consideration to the design of the door. Does the lower section have solid timber panels built into the framework, or is it a glass or plywood panel held by beading? The latter can easily be removed and access gained no matter how many locks are fitted. Door designs are discussed fully in Chapter 3 (see page 37), but if you have any doubt about the suitability of a door in security terms I advise you to visit your local stockist for advice and look at the possibility of buying a new door.

4

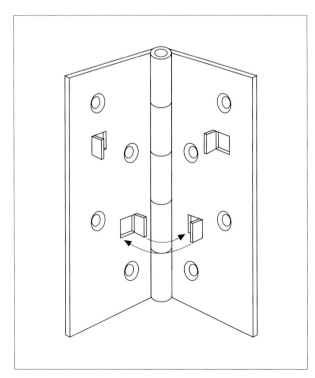

Fig 1.1 Security hinge with interlocking lugs.

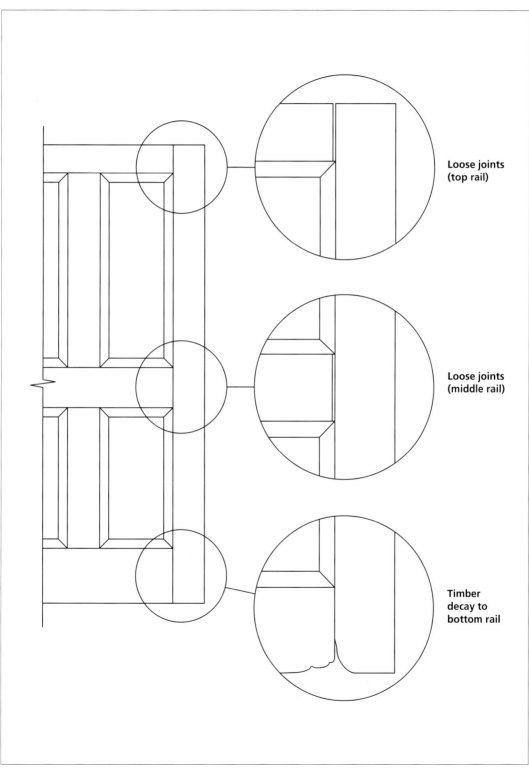

Loose joints
(top rail)

Loose joints
(middle rail)

5

Timber
decay to
bottom rail

Fig 1.2 Check the top, middle and bottom rail joints of the door.

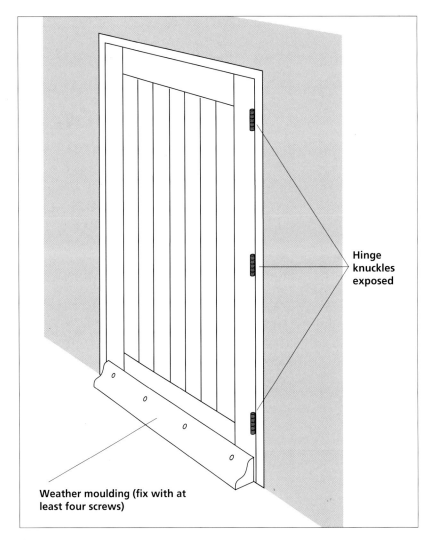

Fig 1.3 An external door that opens outwards, exposing the hinge knuckles. A typical weather moulding is also shown here, and these should always be secured with at least four screws.

Hinge knuckles exposed

Weather moulding (fix with at least four screws)

Most doors open *into* the property as you enter, but it is not unheard of for the door to open outwards. If this is the case, you will notice that the knuckle of the hinge protrudes into the open air (see Fig 1.3). While such hinges are normally made of brass or cast iron to reduce the effects of weathering, they are still vulnerable to potential intruders. Brass hinges have a stainless steel pin to pivot the knuckle and this can be removed easily to gain access. The knuckles of cast iron hinges can be smashed into fragments with a well-placed blow from a hammer. Such

doors should be fitted with security lug hinges or hinge bolts (see Fig 3.14 on page 48).

The position of a door's letterbox is worthy of consideration. Could access be gained by reaching in and turning the latch (see Fig 1.4)? You can see that this door's letterbox is positioned vertically directly below the latch, making access extremely easy if no other locks are there to secure the door further. A door such as this *must* be further secured by a mortise deadlock (these are locks that can only be operated by means of a key (see Fig 1.5).

Fig 1.4 This vertical letterbox, positioned as it is directly beneath the latch, makes access incredibly easy unless the latch is deadlocked (see Chapter 8) or the door fitted with an additional mortise deadlock (see Chapter 5).

External doors should be fitted with a minimum of two locks. The first lock might be a security rim latch lock (see Fig 1.6) or a five-lever mortise sash lock, which provides a hand operated latch for general use of the door and a key operated security bolt (see Fig 1.7). Whichever of these two locks you choose, the door should also be fitted with a second lock, this being a mortise deadlock as shown in Fig 1.5.

The 'five lever' element with regard to mortise locks is very important, as the number of levers in the lock dictates how secure it is. Locks with *fewer* than five levers are not normally recognized by insurance companies as a sufficient deterrent to would-be housebreakers. The number

Fig 1.5 Component parts of a mortise deadlock. Full details of how to fit these are given in Chapter 5.

Fig 1.6 A typical security rim latch lock, in this case made by Era.

Fig 1.7 A five-lever mortise sash lock.

Fig 1.8 A five-lever mortise deadlock in place.

of levers in a lock is usually stamped on the lock's face, so check that your existing lock has five or more levers. If the number is not stamped on the lock face, look inside the lock and count the levers (see Chapter 5, page 62, for step-by-step guidance on this).

I would always recommend that security rim latch or mortise sash locks be supported by a five-lever mortise deadlock (see Fig 1.8).

You should also consider further increasing the security of the door by adding tower or hinge bolts, a door chain, a door viewer (often known as 'spyholes'), and possibly deadbolts. The fitting of all these items is covered later in this book.

Finally, remember that an unsecured back gate is an open invitation to intruders. If you have a back gate, have a look to see if the existing fittings provide security for the rear of the house and outbuildings. Look also at any fences around the garden; are they in good order?

If the roof of your home is of clay tiles, you will often find that only one row of tiles in five is

actually nailed to the roof battens. This means that the tiles not nailed down can simply be lifted up and removed to gain access to the building by entering the roof space and dropping down into the house through the loft access cover. (This does not apply to slate roofs as each slate must be nailed to hold it in position.) If you fix steel reinforcing mesh of the type used in concreting to the underside of the rafters, this will deter the average thief. Most suppliers will be glad to cut the sheets of mesh to a manageable size for you, or loan you a pair of bolt cutters to do it yourself. When fixing the mesh to the rafters, *don't* use nails, as the knocking could damage the roof tiles. Use screws and straps to fix the mesh in place (see Fig 1.9).

Fig 1.9 Steel reinforcing mesh fixed to the underside of your roof in the loft space will prevent anyone who has removed tiles from getting any further.

9

As a further precaution, or as a cheaper alternative, fit a lock or catch to the loft access cover.

Ask yourself whether internal door fittings would also reduce the risk of thieves getting into other parts of the house with ease. The structure of internal doors and the options available are covered in Chapter 3.

Assessing the garage

Garages are a favourite target for thieves, as they are uninhabited and full of small items that are easy to steal. The main door to a garage is usually either the traditional wood-framed, ledged and braced wooden door or the metal, 'up-and-over' type (see Fig 1.10).

Wooden garage doors are usually hung on heavy-duty band and gudgeon hinges (see Fig 1.11), whereas a rear or side access door to the garage may be hung on lighter T hinges (see Fig 1.12). Look to see if the fixings holding the hinges in place are screws, bolts or a combination of both. Make a note of this, and sketch the hinges and the

Fig 1.10 Two typical types of garage door.

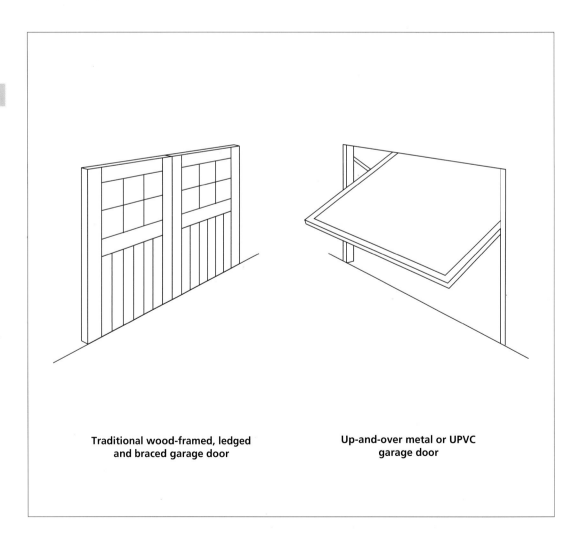

Traditional wood-framed, ledged and braced garage door

Up-and-over metal or UPVC garage door

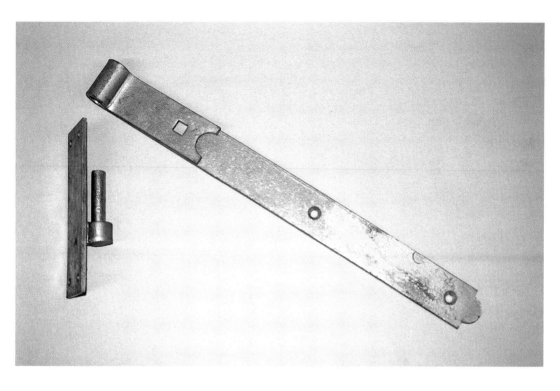

Fig 1.11 Heavy-duty band and gudgeon hinges, commonly used to hang traditional wooden garage doors.

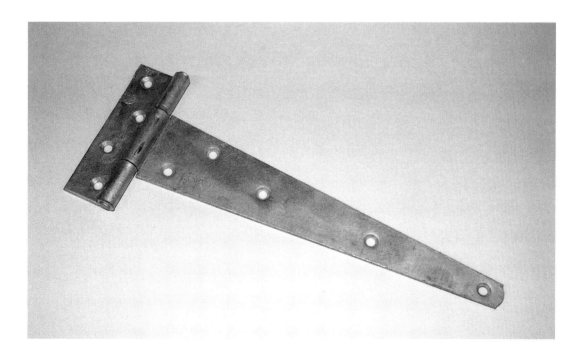

Fig 1.12 A garage side door would normally be hung on a relatively light T hinge like this.

position of any bolts fully penetrating the door and frame. Also, check to see if the backs of the bolts are supported by washers or a metal plate (see Fig 1.13). Compare your findings with the recommendations given in the relevant chapter.

The up-and-over metal or UPVC garage doors usually make an unacceptable amount of noise for a thief, but if the central lock is the only one, you may want to further secure the door. Do *not* fit an additional lock to the door if the door is fitted with remote control opening, as this will damage the motor when you try to open the door. Contact the door supplier for advice on upgrading the security of the door.

Ordinary, manual-opening garage doors can easily be secured with a five-lever mortise deadlock which can be bolted to the door edge (see Chapter 5).

Fig 1.13 **Band and gudgeon hinge fixed through the garage door frame with long bolts.**

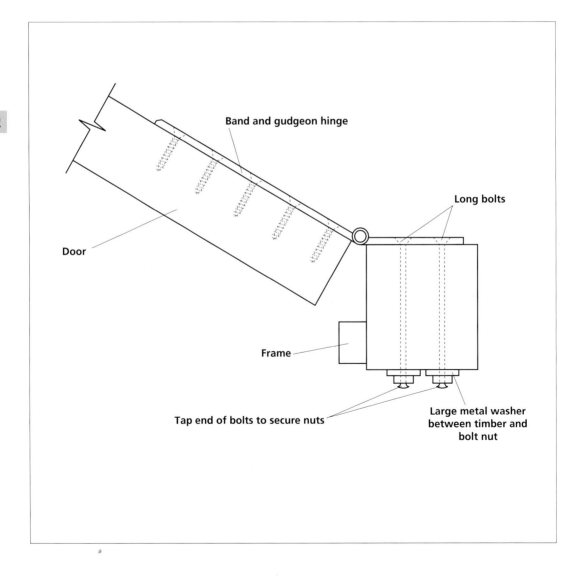

Band and gudgeon hinge

Long bolts

Door

Frame

Tap end of bolts to secure nuts

Large metal washer between timber and bolt nut

Securing windows

2

It is useful to have a basic understanding of the terminology used to identify the various types of window frame and their parts in order to appreciate how they may best be secured and to assist you when visiting a supplier. The following section describes the sectional shapes of opening sash windows and shows the best positions for security locks to be fitted.

Wooden casement windows

These are standard casement window frames with two opening sashes, one top-hung and one side-hung. The head, jamb and sill form the perimeter of the frame and we will look at these first (refer to Fig 2.1).

Perimeter sections

Head
The head is the uppermost section of the window frame. On the example frame shown in Fig 2.1, the smaller sash is hinged into the head and is referred to as a top-hung sash.

Jamb
The jamb refers to the two vertical sides of a window frame. The larger opening sash in the example frame is hinged into the jamb and is referred to as a side-hung sash.

Sill

This is the largest section of timber in the construction of a window frame. It is grooved at the rear to take the internal window board and extended at the front to allow water to drip clear of the brickwork.

Timber sections within the perimeter

Now you are familiar with the parts of the perimeter of the frame, you need to know a little about the timber sections *within* the

perimeter, which separate the opening sashes and the fixed glass panels. There are three main elements here.

Mullion

This refers to the vertical, commonly middle member of the window frame, dividing main (in this case two) panes, or 'lights' (see Fig 2.1).

Transom

This refers to the horizontal member of a window frame, in this case separating the lower, fixed light from the upper, opening, top-hung sash.

Fig 2.1 Parts of a stormproof casement window.

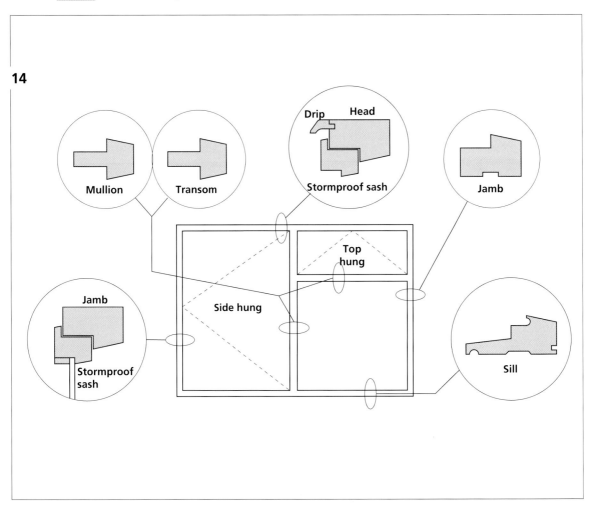

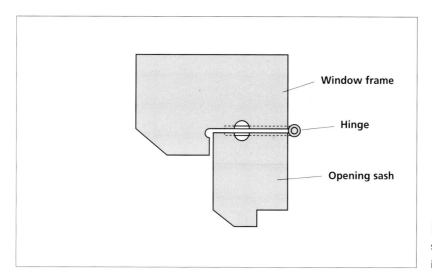

Fig 2.2 Traditional, square sashes sit fully into the rebate.

Opening sashes

The two sashes are the elements of the window that need to be properly secured against break-in. The position of the hinges is indicated by the dotted line symbol shown in Fig 2.1. In this case, the small top light is hinged at its top (head) and main window on the left-hand side (jamb).

The type of hinge used is governed by the section of the framing used. This may be either a traditional square sash, which sits fully into the frame rebate (see Fig 2.2), or a stormproof sash which is brought forward slightly, reducing the main rebate depth but providing an extra external overlap of timber on the outside which increases the ability of the frame to resist the effects of bad weather (see Fig 2.3). In either case the internal position of a security fitting is the same.

15

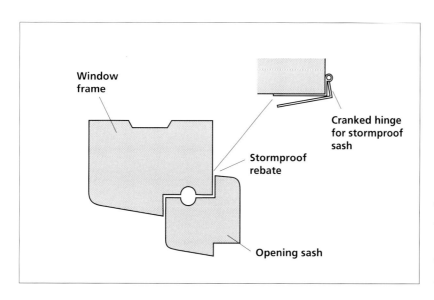

Fig 2.3 A stormproof sash. You can see how these are 'brought forward' to allow protection against the weather by means of an external rebate.

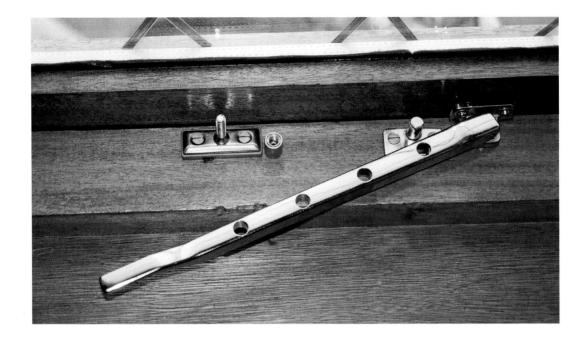

Fig 2.4 **A simple locking pin will secure the casement stay of sash windows.**

16

Casement security

Top sash

The small top sash may be difficult to climb through, but is often easy to open from the outside by means of a well-placed blow with the fist against the middle of the transom, thus causing the window stay to spring from its holding pins. To remove the risk of the top-hung sash being sprung open in such a way, the casement stay should have a locking pin or be upgraded by fitting a variety of security locks.

Fitting a locking pin

If the window stay has holes designed to receive a fixed pin through the arm, then a replacement, locking pin will effectively upgrade the fitting (see Fig 2.4). Simply remove one of the existing pins and replace it with the new locking pin. If the window frame has a chamfered (sloping) section,

you will first need to fit the tapered plastic seating pieces provided with the fitting in order to give the new pin a level surface. If the existing screw holes prove to be a nuisance by pulling the new fitting to one side or the other, remove the locking pin and plug the existing holes with a piece of wood, then re-screw the locking pin in the required position. Finally, screw the locking nut in position with the security key provided.

Fitting a locking bar

If the existing stay does not have holes in it for locking pins to pass through, as the locking pins locate into the underside of the stay, then you will need to fit what is known as a locking bar, or window-stay bolt. Here, a locking bar slides over the top of the existing stay, thus effectively restricting its movement (see Figs 2.5 and 2.6). This fitting is designed to replace the existing pin, but you could refit this further back towards the stay's pivot point for additional stability (see Fig 2.7).

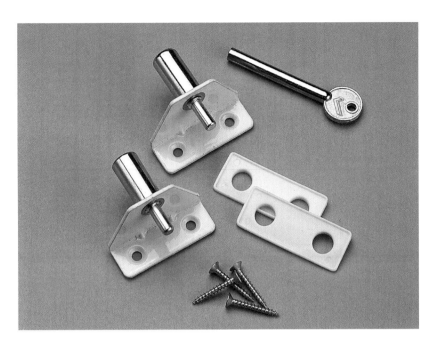

Fig 2.5 A window-stay kit.

Fig 2.6 (below) A locking bar with key from the same kit.

17

To fit the new locking bar, remove the existing pin and position the new fitting in its place. Once in position, have a look to see if the screw holes in the frame line up with the holes in the new fitting. If they do, fix the lock with the screws provided. If the holes don't line up, you will need to plug them with

Fig 2.7 (below) Two pins provide extra stability, and mean you do not waste the original pin when you fit a new security pin.

Fig 2.8 Here the holes of the old and new pins did not line up, so the old holes needed to be plugged. Spent matchsticks work as well as anything else in these instances.

timber (see Fig 2.8). Once again, if the frame is chamfered in section, use the tapered plastic seating pieces to level up the fitting prior to fixing.

To refit the old pin further back along the stay, lift the arm of the stay and place the old pin in a position that will locate into the underside of the arm and bring the arm down to the locking position. If the fitting is sitting squarely on the frame and its rectangular base is parallel with the arm of the stay, mark the front face and one end of the base as a guide to the fixing position. If the fitting is not sitting flat you may be able to use a spare plastic taper to level it, if you have one. If not, you may have to set the pin into the frame to get it level. However, some pins are

manufactured with a tapered base, so turn the pin around and see if this alters the angle. If the pin doesn't have a tapered base and is still not sitting flat, position it against the two pencil marks you have already made, and draw around its base with a sharp pencil. Then use a sharp chisel to cut the two end lines across the grain, making sure that the chisel remains vertical and does not go beyond the pencil lines to either side or below the front face pencil mark (see Fig 2.9). Next, gently cut along the back pencil line staying within the perimeter lines. You will find that the chisel will sink into the timber much more easily when cutting the back line as you will be cutting with the grain, so take care not to go too deep. Finally, hold the chisel parallel with

18

Fig 2.9 (right) Do not cut beyond the pencil lines at the sides or cut below the front face pencil mark.

the window board (see Fig 2.10) and cut the chamfer from zero depth at the front to the required depth at the rear to achieve a level area for the pin to sit on. Once you have positioned the pin, use a square-point bradawl to make a pilot hole. A square-point bradawl breaks the wood grain rather than parting it as would a pointed bradawl, and avoids any splitting in the wood when the screws are put in. Now screw the pin firmly in place.

Main (side) sash

Side-hung sashes are secured both at the base with a casement stay and on the vertical opening side of the sash with what is known as a lever or

Fig 2.10 (below) Hold the chisel parallel with the window board to accurately level off the chamfer.

'cockspur' handle (see Fig 2.11). If only one lever handle is fitted to the sash, close the window and push gently at the top and bottom of the frame from the inside to see if there is any movement outwards. If you find that you can move the sash, it is wise to fit security locks above and below the lever handle, approximately 150mm (6in) from the top and bottom of the sash.

There are numerous types of fittings available to secure a side-hung wooden sash, but here we will look at three different locks: the casement window snap lock; the pivot lock; and the security bolt.

Casement window snap lock

The casement window snap lock (see Fig 2.12) is a very effective unit, as well as being simple to use. It is easy to fit, using only a chisel-point bradawl and a screwdriver. With the window closed, hold the lock against the frame in its intended position with the key position facing you and the larger screw holes visible when in place. Mark the position of the three faces adjacent to the sash to

20

Fig 2.11 **A 'cockspur' or 'lever' handle on a side-hung window.**

Fig 2.12 **A casement window snap-lock kit.**

Fig 2.13 **Hold the lock in place and mark its position on the frame.**

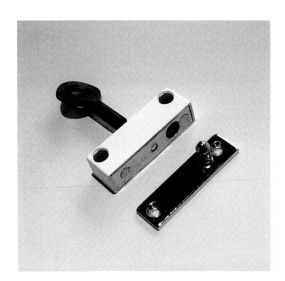

Fig 2.14 If the window is hinged on the right, make sure the striking plate and the pin are at the top, as here.

Fig 2.15 If the window is hinged on the left, the striking plate and pin should be at the bottom.

21

give the position to fix the striking plate (see Fig 2.13). You will notice that the pin which is fixed to the striking plate is off-centre and as the fitting is designed to fit clockwise and anti-clockwise openings, this will affect which way up you fix the striking plate. If the sash is hinged on the right as you look at it from the inside, then the striking plate and pin should be at the top when fitted (see Fig 2.14). If the sash is hinged on the left, the plate and pin should be at the bottom (see Fig 2.15). With the sash closed, hold the striking plate against the sash in the intended position, at the intersection of the sash and the mullion, as shown in Fig 2.15. Use a chisel-point bradawl to make pilot holes for the fixing screws.

Once you have fixed the striking plate into position, place the snap lock over the pin and slide a piece of card in between the striking plate and the snap lock to reduce the amount of free play when the lock is closed (see Fig 2.16). Then push the bradawl through the two holes in the snap lock and fix it with the screws provided. As with the top-hung sash, use the plastic taper provided if the frame is chamfered.

A gentle twist with the key in either direction will now open the window, but the lock will

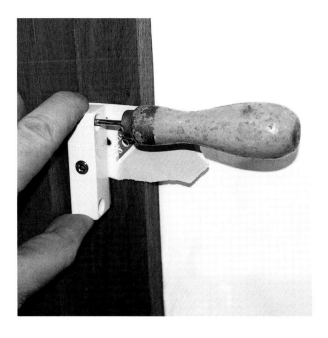

Fig 2.16 Fixing the snap lock into position.

Fig 2.17 A pivot lock.

Fig 2.18 Hold the angled striking plate against the edge of the frame, flush with the edge of the rebate, ready to mark the pilot holes.

22

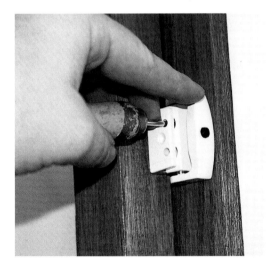

Fig 2.19 With the striking plate fixed, place the lock over it with the window shut, and mark the fixing points with the bradawl.

automatically operate again when the window is closed. This is a very effective unit, and simple to use.

Pivot lock

This lock is also easy to fit, and again requires only a chisel-point bradawl and screwdriver to fix (see Fig 2.17). Open the window and hold the angled striking plate against the edge of the frame, flush with the edge of the rebate (see Fig

2.18). Use the bradawl to create pilot holes, and fix the striking plate to the frame. Close the window, place the lock over the striking plate, and mark the fixing points with the bradawl through the holes in the striking plate (see Fig 2.19). Open the window again, hold the lock in the marked position, and fix it with the screws provided. Now close the window and test the pivot bar for smooth operation. The window is now easily secured by turning the grub screw clockwise.

Security bolt

If you require a more concealed unit and are confident enough to use a few more tools, a security bolt is a good choice (see Fig 2.20). Measure the width of the sash frame to determine the length of the bolt required. You will need a carpenters' brace, appropriately-sized auger bits, normally 9 and 18mm (⅜ and ¾in), a chisel-point bradawl, a chisel for cutting the timber to set in the faceplate, and a screwdriver.

Before you begin, place the bolt against the side of the open sash to double-check that the sash is deep enough to take the depth of the bolt (see Fig 2.21). If you find that there is a serious risk to the glass panel then you will need to get a shorter bolt or use one of the surface-mounted fittings discussed earlier instead. Assuming the

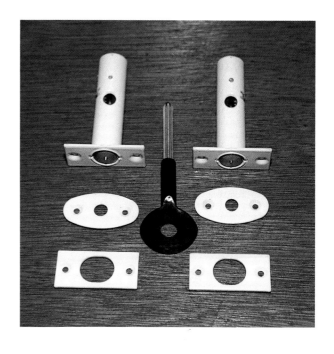

Fig 2.20 **(above) Two security bolts and a key.**

23

Glass

Putty

Security bolt

Insulation tape

Auger

Maximum depth of cut

Fig 2.21 **Check the depth of the bolt against the sash to ensure there is enough depth of wood to receive it. Then measure the required depth of hole and mark the auger bit with insulation tape to act as a depth gauge.**

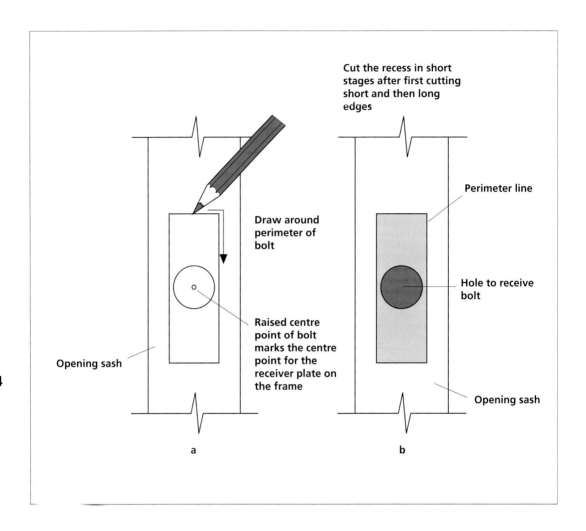

Fig 2.22 Mark and cut the recess for the faceplate.

bolt is not too long, wrap a piece of insulation tape around the auger to mark the required depth of hole (see Fig 2.21). Now drill a hole of the appropriate diameter to take the barrel of the bolt. With the bolt placed in the hole, hold the faceplate parallel with the edge of the sash and use a sharp pencil to draw around the perimeter (see Fig 2.22a). Use a chisel to remove the timber within 'the perimeter line to provide a recess for the faceplate (see Fig 2.22b). Now hold the bolt against the inner face of the sash in line with the faceplate recess and mark the key position with

the bradawl (see Fig 2.23). Now use the 9mm (⅜in) auger to drill through the inner face of the sash, after which you can fit the lock with the screws provided and try the key.

Now fit the escutcheon (key plate). I find the easiest way to do this is to slide the plate onto the key and put the key into the lock. The key plate will spin freely and will need to be turned to a horizontal or vertical position, whichever you wish, prior to fixing with the screws. Fix the screws with the key in place as this will ensure that the hole in the plate lines up well with the hole in the lock.

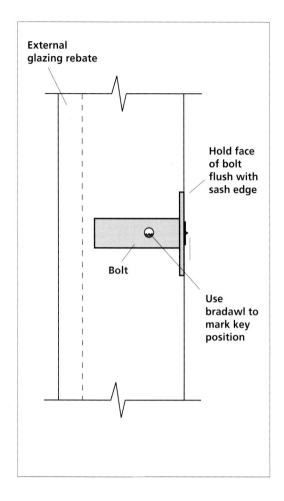

Fig 2.23 Mark the key position on the sash.

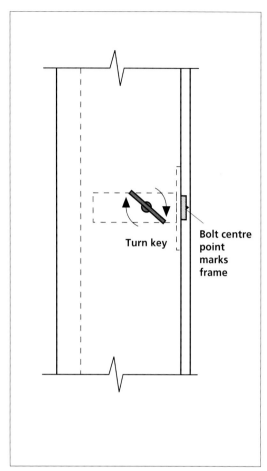

Fig 2.24 Use the centre point on the bolt to mark the position of the receiver hole on the frame.

25

Now drill the receiver hole and fit the receiver plate. If you look closely at the end of the bolt you will notice a raised point (see Fig 2.22a). This point is designed to mark the auger position for drilling the hole to receive the bolt. Close the window and turn the key so that the bolt centre point comes into contact with the window frame opposite and marks it (see Fig 2.24). Open the window and use the 18mm (¾in) auger bit to drill a hole to accept the bolt. Then hold the receiver plate over the hole you have drilled and set it into the frame in the same manner as for the faceplate of the bolt.

Safety

If a side-hung sash could be the only means of escape in case of fire, you must be sure to keep any security keys required to open it close to hand at all times, and make sure all the occupants of the house are familiar with the lock's operation. A further precaution in this respect is to invest in a 'break-glass' emergency escape tool, as shown in Fig 2.25. The bulbous end of the tool conceals a sharp point which comes into contact with the glass when pressed against it, allowing you to break even

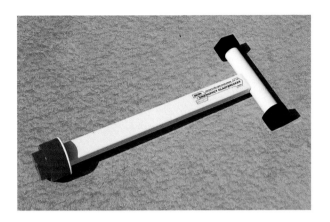

Fig 2.25 'Break-glass' emergency escape tool.

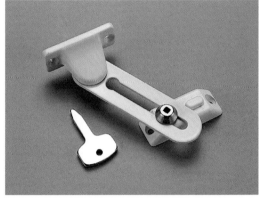

Fig 2.26 Nursery window lock kit.

toughened glass if needed. Follow the tool's instructions carefully, always clear away as much glass as possible after using the tool, and place a blanket over the window sill before climbing out.

Nursery window locks

If you require some ventilation in a room but also need the opening to be secure, a nursery window lock is the answer (see Fig 2.26). This type of lock allows you to open a window a little and still have a measure of security.

With the window closed, place the lock at the front (window edge) of the casement stay (see Fig 2.27). Use the fitting key to slacken off the locking screw, and slide the upper half of the fitting along until you can see both fixing holes of the lock baseplate through the slide groove (see Fig 2.28).

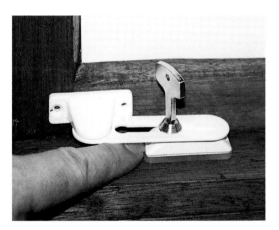

Fig 2.27 Position the lock as shown.

Fig 2.28 With the lock still in position, slide the upper half of the fitting along until you can see the fixing holes in the baseplate (the lock has been removed from the window here so that you can see the holes clearly). Note also the raised lug on the left.

26

Position the fitting so that it touches both the frame and the sash squarely and use a bradawl to start the baseplate holes. If the frame is chamfered, use the angled plastic baseplate provided to level up the fitting.

Now fix the lock baseplate onto the frame and slide the upper half of the fitting back to its original position against the raised lug on the top of the baseplate (you can see the lug clearly in Fig 2.28). The upper section is now ready to fix to the opening sash with the screws provided. Now simply undo the lock with the key and lock it in the open position to check it is operating correctly.

Securing glazing bead

It would be rather pointless to fit security locks to all the opening lights if all a thief has to do is remove the glazing bead and take out the whole pane of glass. There are three options here.

1 Remove the bead and fit security clips to stop the glass being removed, then return the bead to its place. If you can't find a stockist for the clips, you can easily make your own by buying a short length of stainless steel or galvanized metal bent at an angle of 90° to form an L-shape, which is smaller than the bead (see Fig 2.29). Divide the length of metal into four parts, each approximately 25mm (1in) long. Don't cut it yet! It is easier to prepare the clips while they are still joined together. Mark a mid-point on each section, and drill these out to allow for a security screw to fix each clip to the frame (see Fig 2.30).

27

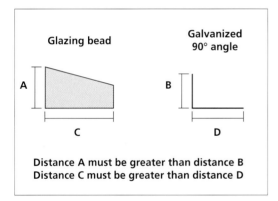

Glazing bead

Galvanized 90° angle

A

B

C

D

Distance A must be greater than distance B
Distance C must be greater than distance D

Fig 2.29 **Make sure the galvanized angle you buy is smaller, both vertically and horizontally, than the glazing bead.**

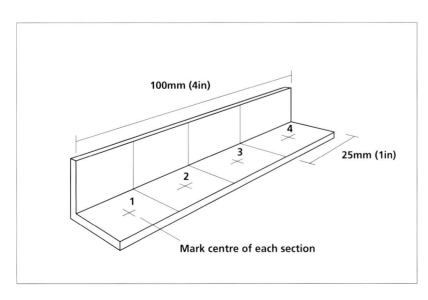

100mm (4in)

1 2 3 4

25mm (1in)

Mark centre of each section

Fig 2.30 **Divide the section into four equal lengths, mark a mid-point on each, and drill holes for the fixing screws.**

Take great care when drilling and use a vice, otherwise the length of metal will try to spin with the drill bit and could cause you injury. Make sure the length of metal is firmly held in the vice and drill the screw holes. Then cut the galvanized angle into the marked lengths. The clips are now ready to fix in place. Remove the glass bead and hold the clip against the frame and the glass, close to the corners of the window. Fix the clips with 25mm (1in) no. 6

gauge stainless steel or brass security screws and refit the beads on a bed of silicone frame sealant which will seal out the weather but not permanently bond the bead to the frame. Sealant comes in tubes and can be applied direct from the tube or by using a 'sealer gun'. All these items are readily available from DIY stores. Security clips form a second line of defence against a burglar who is prepared to remove the beading, without the need to bond the beading permanently to the frame, as in the third option, below.

2 The bead itself can be upgraded with security screws which, once fitted, can't easily be removed as the head of each screw is designed to turn clockwise only. If this method is chosen you need to pre-drill the screw holes to avoid splitting the beading. This method is not very attractive to look at, but you can fit brass screw cups with the screws which will improve the appearance a little.

3 Remove the beading and put it back in place on a bed of woodbonding adhesive mastic which is available at any good DIY or trade supplier. Remember that if you choose option two or three and need to replace the glass at some time in the future, the bead will be completely destroyed when removing it. However, as glazing bead is not very expensive the small cost of replacement is worth the peace of mind that secure glass beading will give.

Vertical sliding box frame sash windows

These windows have a hollow box frame on both sides which is home to the balance weights, hence the name (see Figs 2.31 and 2.32). The weights are connected to the sliding sash by

Fig 2.31 A newly-constructed vertical sliding box frame sash window.

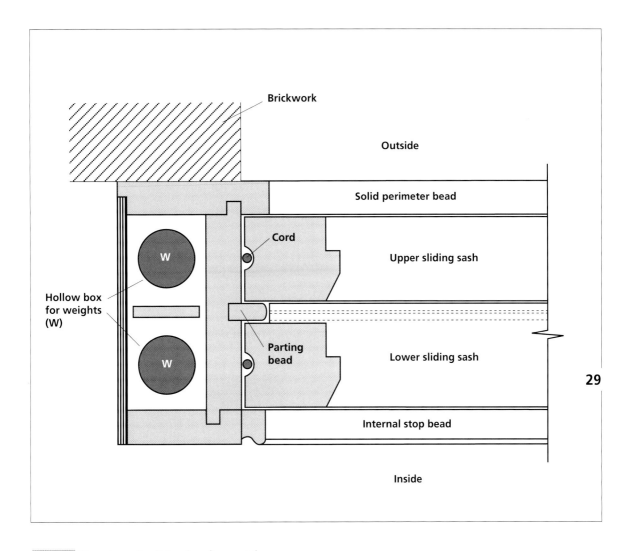

Fig 2.32 Plan view of a sliding box frame sash window showing one of the hollow 'boxes' constructed to hold the counterweights.

means of a waxed cord, and allow the lower frame to stay in the open position, and the upper frame to stay in the closed position. Without them the top frame would crash down and hit the sill.

Vertical sliding box frame sash windows tend to become more vulnerable with age due to their simple operating lock (see Fig 2.33) and the way the two meeting rails are designed

Fig 2.33 An example of a sliding sash window lock.

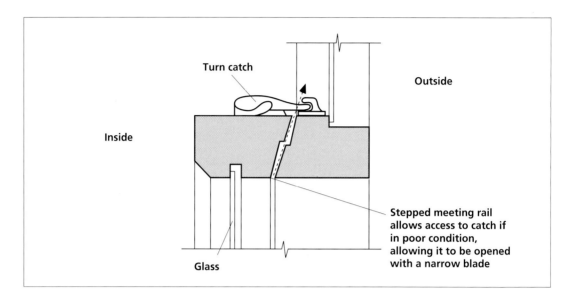

Fig 2.34 Cross-section of the meeting rails of a sliding sash window showing the potential for break-in if the window is old and secured only by a 'turn catch' lock.

30

Fig 2.35 (right) A simple meeting rail lock.

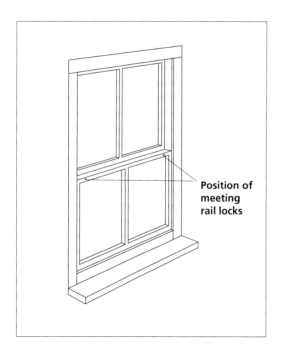

Position of meeting rail locks

Fig 2.36 Suggested location of meeting rail locks.

(see Fig 2.34). However, if properly secured, box frame sash windows are in some respects less vulnerable to intruders than casement windows. First, they have no vulnerable external beading, as the sliding sash frames are fitted and beaded in place from the inside. Second, the glass is held in the frame by putty, not glass beading, which when set is more time consuming to remove than glazing bead, thus making removing the glass a less attractive option.

A simple lock fitted to the meeting rail of a sliding box frame sash window will effectively

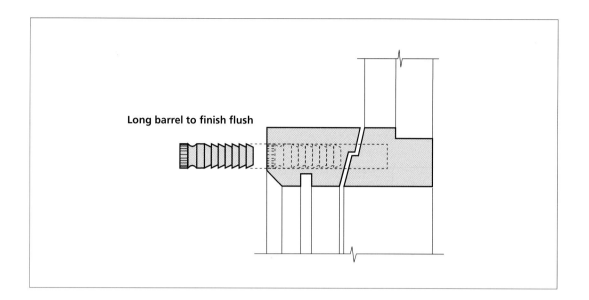

Fig 2.37 (above) Slide in the long barrel to finish flush with the frame.

Fig 2.38 (below) Raise the window and tap the short barrel into the hole in the outer frame.

upgrade its security (see Fig 2.35). I recommend you fit two of these locks to each frame in the positions indicated in Fig 2.36. To do the job, you will need only a 9.5mm (⅜in) auger, a mallet and possibly a junior hacksaw.

Fitting a meeting rail lock

Make sure that the window is fully closed and held firm by the existing catch. Next, mark the point for drilling a 9.5mm (⅜in) hole. This needs to be drilled right through the meeting rail of the inner frame and 19mm (¾in) into the outer meeting rail. Measure the width of the outer rail and add 19mm (¾in), giving you the overall depth required. Mark this on the auger with insulating tape as a depth-guide to ensure you do not drill too deep. Remove the locking pin from the longer barrel and tap the longer barrel into the inner frame (see Fig 2.37). Open the window so you can see the holes you have drilled into the outer frame and gently tap the shorter barrel into the hole, making sure it is fully home (see Fig 2.38).

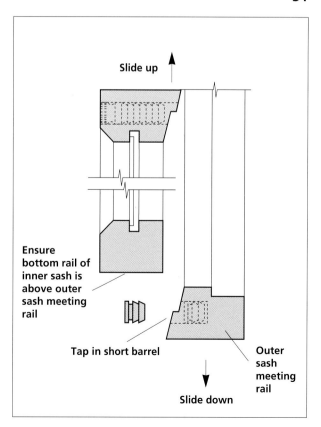

Close the window and slide the locking pin into the inner barrel, until it meets the locking thread within the barrel, and then turn the pin clockwise to lock the pin into the two halves of the fitting. When you have done this you may find that the square head of the pin is sticking out of the barrel, so you will need to reduce the length of the pin by the amount that it is proud. Make sure that you cut the correct end of the bolt, i.e. not the threaded head. Use a junior hacksaw to cut the pin to the correct length and refit it into the barrel.

Metal window frames

More recently-made metal window frames are usually constructed from aluminium, but older frames tend to be made of iron.

Iron frames

The casement stays and cockspur handles of iron-framed windows are often welded into position and are very difficult to remove and replace. It is far simpler to upgrade the existing fittings than to try and replace them. Iron frames of the multi-pane Georgian style are vulnerable because an intruder only has to break a small pane of glass to gain access to both the cockspur handle and the casement stay. If the cockspur handle is restrained by means of a locking bolt, the vulnerability of the design can be overcome. Fig 2.39 shows a unit which is very simple to fit, the only tools needed being an 8mm (⅜in) open-end or ring spanner and a small flat file. The bolt fits into the fork on the handle, which ensures the window is secure, but

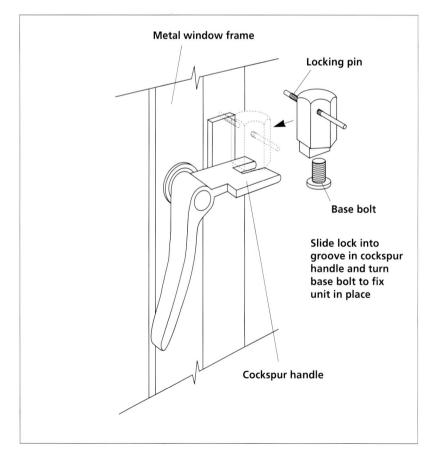

Metal window frame

Locking pin

Base bolt

Slide lock into groove in cockspur handle and turn base bolt to fix unit in place

Cockspur handle

Fig 2.39 The correct position for a locking bolt on a cockspur handle.

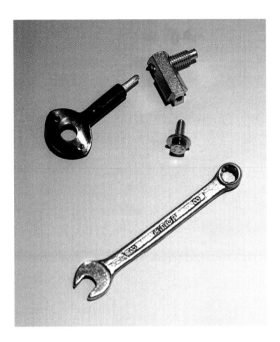

Fig 2.40 Begin by slackening off the pin at the base of the fitting with an appropriately-sized spanner.

Fig 2.41 Turn the locking pin anti-clockwise using the key, so that it is flush with the face of the bolt stem.

33

this will remove the option of using the slotted cockspur handle to hold the frame ajar to provide a small amount of ventilation through the frame. If ventilation is important for the location, then alternative methods to ventilate the room will need to be considered, such as air bricks in the external wall or a ventilation fan in place of a glass panel.

Fitting a cockspur locking bolt

To fit the bolt, slacken off the holding pin at the base of the fitting (see Fig 2.40). Using the key, turn the locking pin anti-clockwise until the end of the pin is flush with the face of the bolt stem (see Fig 2.41). Hold the bolt over the cockspur handle to see if it will locate into the fork as indicated in Fig 2.39. If you have difficulty getting it into position, careful use of the file to ensure a snug fit may be required. Once you have managed to get the bolt in position, use the 8mm (⅜in) spanner to tighten the locking pin at the base, and try the bolt by turning the locking pin clockwise until it touches the frame.

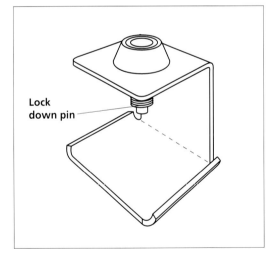

Lock down pin

Fig 2.42 Window-stay clamp.

Another very simple and inexpensive lock suitable for metal windows is the window-stay clamp (see Fig 2.42). This unit requires no tools to fit as it simply clips onto the existing window stay in the closed position, and locks by means of a key to turn a threaded pin down onto the stay.

Aluminium frames

There are many types of surface-mounted lock suitable for aluminium windows and patio doors. In most cases it is necessary to pre-drill pilot holes to take the fitting screws, but sometimes the locks are supplied with self-drilling, self-tapping screws. Unlike timber frames, aluminium frames give very little margin for error if the opposing sides of the lock do not line up accurately, so take care in marking out the fixing positions.

UPVC (plastic) windows

UPVC windows are becoming the most popular replacement frames in Europe, and it is well worth the effort to talk to a number of suppliers in order to gain a full understanding of the products on the market. If a bay window is involved, it is worth paying an independent advisor to confirm the load bearing structural integrity of the frames offered to you before accepting any quotations.

Fig 2.43 Attach double-sided security tape to the inside of the frame rebate.

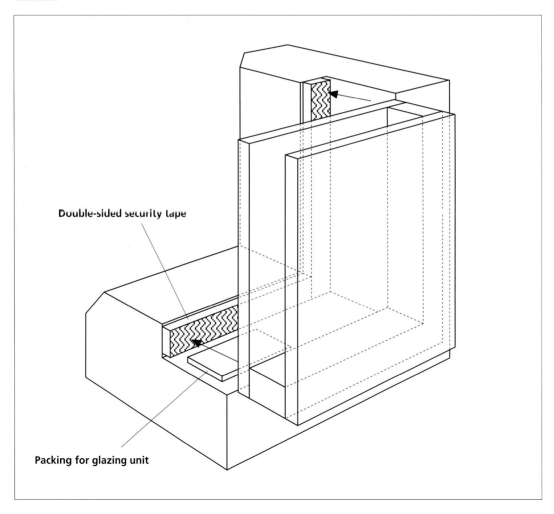

Double-sided security tape

Packing for glazing unit

When discussing purchase of UPVC window units you will be required to decide on a single locking system or a triple shoot bolt locking system. You may pay a little more for the triple shoot bolts, but they are by far the most secure option. You will also need to give thought to the ability of the sash to withstand pressure applied from the outside to try and lever it open; frames should be internally fitted with a galvanized steel box section running through the length of the sash to restrict movement and prevent this.

Choosing UPVC window frames also gives you the option of having glazing units fitted from the *inside* with internal beading, so that there is no vulnerable external bead, again adding to frame security.

If you have already purchased your frames or the existing frames are a legacy of the previous tenant and do not have any of the above-mentioned features, it is not difficult to upgrade the opening sashes substantially by fitting surface-mounted locks similar to those used on the timber or aluminium frames discussed earlier, using self tapping screws to fit the locks. You can also upgrade the security of the glazed units if you feel this is necessary, by using one of the following methods.

1 If the UPVC frame is externally beaded, remove the glazing bead, which is usually quite easy to spring out from the middle of its length by pressing it against the glass and twisting away from the frame. Remember that such glazed units are often very heavy, so enlist the help of a friend to remove it. Now fit a perimeter run of double-sided security tape to the inside of the frame rebate, as shown in Fig 2.43. If the glazing unit was sitting on packing before removal, make sure these are back in place before putting the unit back into the frame (see Fig 2.43). The security tape will not allow you to manoeuvre the glazing unit once contact between the two surfaces has been made, so make sure you are

35

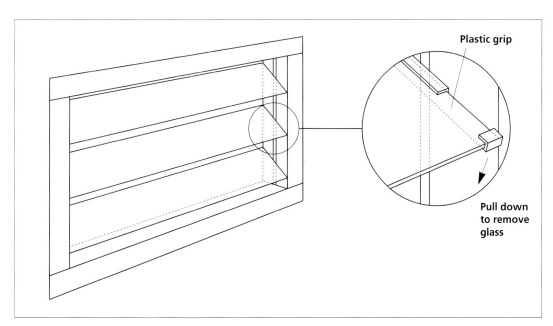

Plastic grip

Pull down to remove glass

Fig 2.44 Louvre windows like this are a very high security risk.

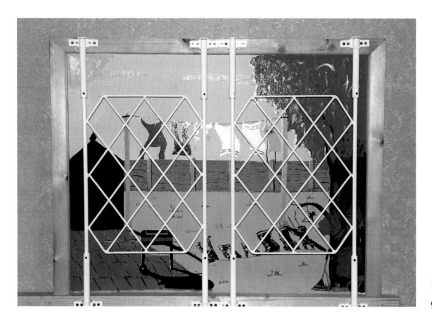

Fig 2.45 Security grids for windows.

36

happy with the perimeter margin before pressing the unit into place. Now replace the external beading to complete the job.

2 If you know the manufacturer's name, you could contact them and ask if they could supply you with purpose-made security clips which can be fitted under the beading as per their instructions.

Louvre window slats

Louvre windows such as the type illustrated in Fig 2.44 present a very high security risk. The best option here is to replace the whole unit with a new wooden or UPVC frame. If this is not possible then you must at least attempt to upgrade the louvre blades by gluing them in place using a time-bond adhesive. This will give you the chance to slide the glass blades into the plastic clips before the glue takes a grip.

If you look closely at the plastic pivoting clip holding the glass in place (see Fig 2.44), you will see that by applying downward pressure to the extreme lower end you can bend the plastic clip, which will allow you to slide the glass towards you and remove it. If possible it is also a good idea to fit a purpose-built metal security grid, as shown in Fig 2.45.

Securing doors

3

A s with windows, it is good to have a basic understanding of the design and construction of doors, as this will help you to understand why certain security measures are as effective as they are. Unfortunately, forced entry remains a possibility even when a good quality security lock has been fitted, so extra security devices are recommended, even on good quality doors.

External wooden doors are normally constructed from a solid perimeter frame and a choice of infill panel designs (see Fig 3.1). Although the perimeter can be secured, this would be pointless if access could be achieved by removing one of the door panels and climbing in without even looking at the security locks.

Door construction

The perimeter of an external door is normally made up of a top rail, bottom rail and two sides, known as stiles (see Fig 3.1). The stiles can also be individually identified as the hanging stile (hinge side) and the locking stile which houses the locks and supports the door furniture (handles). The location of each stile is determined by the opening hand of the door (clockwise or anti-clockwise – see Fig 3.2) and

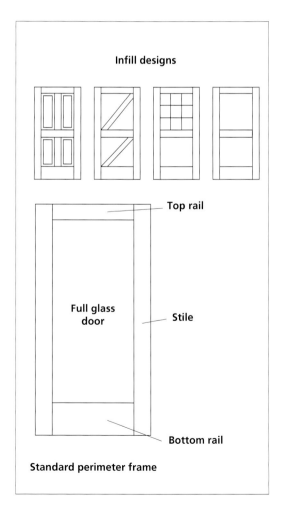

Infill designs

Top rail

Full glass door

Stile

Bottom rail

Standard perimeter frame

Fig 3.1 Doors normally consist of a standard perimeter frame, with a variety of infill designs.

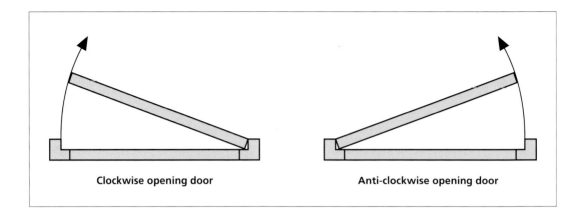

Clockwise opening door   Anti-clockwise opening door

Fig 3.2 (above) Doors can be hung to open clockwise or anti-clockwise.

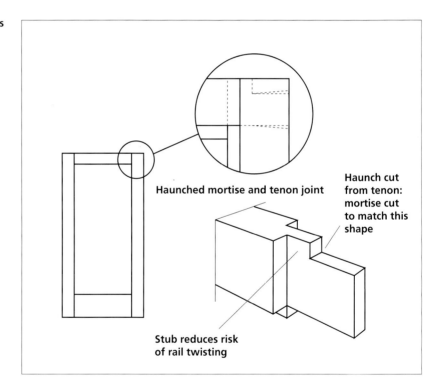

Haunched mortise and tenon joint

Haunch cut from tenon: mortise cut to match this shape

Stub reduces risk of rail twisting

Fig 3.3 Through mortise and tenon joint.

doesn't mean that the two stiles differ in any way in size or shape.

The traditional woodworking joint used to form the four corners of a door is the through mortise and tenon (see Fig 3.3), which is 'haunched' at the joint's outer edge. This means that the tenon is cut back to allow a section of the mortise in the door stile to remain intact and lock the joint in place. The short stub section of the tenon also gives the tenoned rail stability by reducing the risk of twist. If the joint was not haunched in this fashion it would simply slide out of the mortise sideways.

A more modern manufacturing method used to construct doors is the use of timber dowels

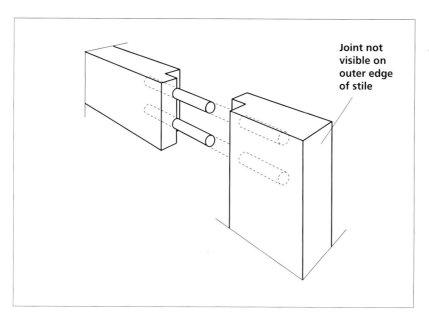

Joint not
visible on
outer edge
of stile

Fig 3.4 Modern dowel joint.

(round pins), fitted into the horizontal rails which line up with holes drilled into the stiles (see Fig 3.4). When fitting security locks to such doors, there is a risk of reducing the strength of the joint by cutting into the dowel (for example, when drilling a hole for a security dead bolt). Guidance is given on the correct technique to avoid this on page 46.

If you look at the edge of a door you can usually tell if it has been constructed using traditional through mortise and tenon joints or timber dowels, as the ends of traditional tenons should be visible. If dowel joints were used, no joints will be visible on the door edge (see Fig 3.4).

Door panel weak points

It is important to identify whether the panels were built into the frame during manufacture, or held in place by timber beading, the latter being far more vulnerable (see Fig 3.5).

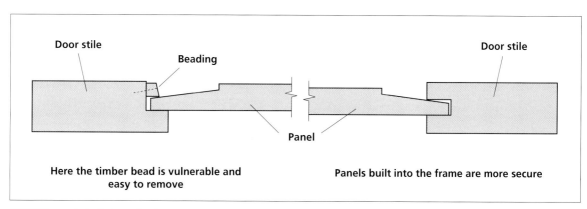

Door stile

Beading

Door stile

Panel

Here the timber bead is vulnerable and
easy to remove

Panels built into the frame are more secure

Fig 3.5 Panels built into the frame (right) are more secure than those held in place by timber beading (left).

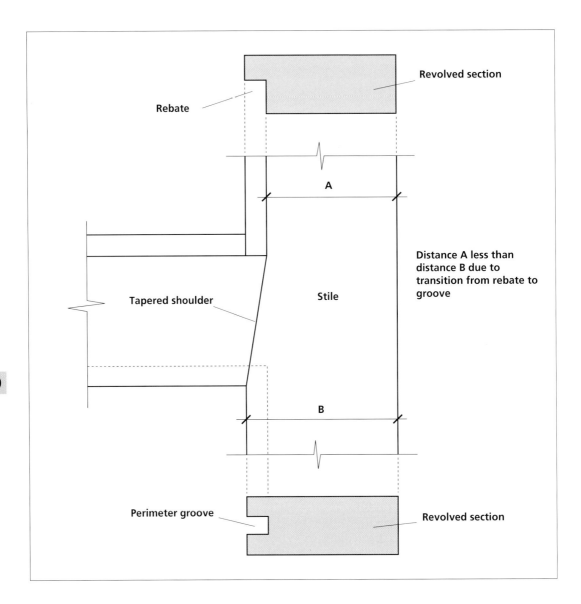

Revolved section

Rebate

A

Distance A less than distance B due to transition from rebate to groove

Tapered shoulder

Stile

B

Perimeter groove

Revolved section

40

Fig 3.6 **The gunstock shoulder – a traditional joint used to transfer from a grooved to a rebated stile.**

If the door has a plywood panel in the lower half, check whether the panel is held in place by timber beading. If so, you will need to upgrade the beading. This will also give you the opportunity to increase the thickness of the plywood panel before returning the beading to its place.

Even if the plywood panel is held in place by a perimeter groove in the rails and stiles (and hence fitted during construction), it is a good idea

to check the strength of the plywood panel. Press the centre of the panel and feel for movement. If the panel moves when pressed, upgrade it by placing an additional ply panel against the existing panel, holding it in place with secure timber beading.

If you can't immediately tell whether the panel is held by a perimeter groove or rebate and timber bead, a tell-tale sign of transferring from a rebate where timber beading is required to a groove can be seen by examination of the door stiles (see Fig 3.6). A traditional method of carrying out the transfer from rebate to groove is by means of a tapering shoulder on the rail tenon called a gunstock shoulder: notice the general shape of the stile is similar to a rifle butt (see Fig 3.6). This traditional method of tapering a tenon shoulder was often used in the past to reduce the overall width of wide door stiles in order to increase the light from upper glazed panels.

If your door has moulded timber panels, once again check to see if they are held in place by timber beading or by grooves in the frame. Moulded panels are usually built into a door during manufacture, and hence are fairly secure, but if they *are* held by timber beading they will be very easy to remove. Do not be concerned if you discover that you can move a moulded panel slightly from side to side; such panels are never glued into their grooves, to allow for the natural expansion and contraction of the timber in hot and cold weather.

It may be that the panels are not made of timber at all. They are often manufactured from more stable (inert) material such as medium density fibreboard (MDF) which will not split as timber panels frequently do.

Framed ledged and braced doors

These doors are constructed using v-jointed tongue and grooved boards (refer to Fig 1.3 on page 6). Even with security locks fitted to the door stiles, such doors remain vulnerable because the v-jointed boards on the face of the door can be removed. Therefore, you need to improve the security of the boards before deciding which lock to fit. There are several options here.

If there is a weather moulding fitted at the bottom of the door (refer to Fig 1.3 on page 6), it will span the face of all the boards and the door stiles, but is often held in place by only two screws. If you increase the number of screws, you will improve the security of the door. You will need to pre-drill the position of the screws so as not to split the timber, which is especially likely near the ends of the weather moulding.

Where the v-jointed boards meet the top rail, they are chamfered on the return end of the board to match the v-joint. The chamfered end grain leaves them vulnerable to the effects of bad weather. By fitting a 'head drip' you will both protect the end grain and make the door more secure by making it more difficult to remove the v-jointed boards. Make the head drip from any suitable hardwood or softwood, treated with a spirit-based preservative. It should be pre-drilled in the same way as the weather moulding and is simple to make out of a length of 50 x 38mm (2 x 1½in), as shown in Fig 3.7.

Fitting the appropriate lock

Once you have examined your door and upgraded the boarded areas as required you can consider what level of security is needed and where to fit the locks. If the door has only one pair of hinges you will need to upgrade by fitting an additional hinge (see Chapter 4, page 51). An external door should have a minimum of two locks: a mortise deadlock and either a key-operated cylinder latch or a secure sash lock (both known as 'primary locks').

Cylinder latch locks are discussed in Chapter 8. If you prefer a lock with an integrated door handle, choose a sash lock that incorporates a key-operated security bolt with at least five levers. The greater the number of levers, the greater the resistance against the lock being picked, due to the complexity of the key required to operate it.

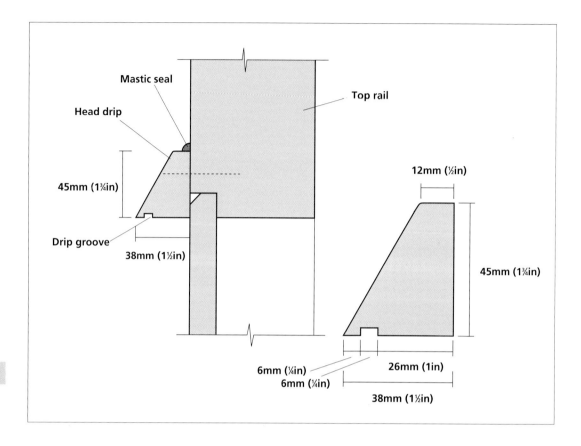

Mastic seal

Head drip

Top rail

12mm (½in)

45mm (1¾in)

45mm (1¾in)

Drip groove

38mm (1½in)

6mm (¼in)

6mm (¼in)

26mm (1in)

38mm (1½in)

Fig 3.7 A head drip.

Whichever primary lock you choose, the door still needs a secondary lock, which is key operated only (i.e. has no latch). Such locks are known as mortise deadlocks (as illustrated in Fig 1.8 on page 8). Fitting a mortise deadlock is very similar to fitting a mortise latch (described in Chapter 5), the only difference being that the mortise deadlock is key-operated and therefore only requires a small escutcheon plate (keyhole plate) fitted to the door face. This is also covered in Chapter 5.

In addition to the minimum two, I recommend you also consider fitting two small deadbolts, which are operated from inside the door, and should be fitted at both the top and bottom of the locking stile. Fitting bolts is fully described later in this chapter, on page 46.

You may also wish to consider fitting hinge bolts into the door frame on the hinge side. These provide a high level of security against hinge tampering, particularly if the door opens outwards. Hinge bolts have no moving parts and operate by means of a fixed pin which locks into a metal receiver in the frame rebate as the door is closed. Fitting hinge bolts is covered later on in this chapter on pages 47–9.

Security doors

It is now possible to purchase doors with a glassfibre or metal outer skin which give a high level of resistance against impact from outside. These doors are available in a variety of designs and natural-effect finishes and can be supplied pre-fitted in their own frame. If you are

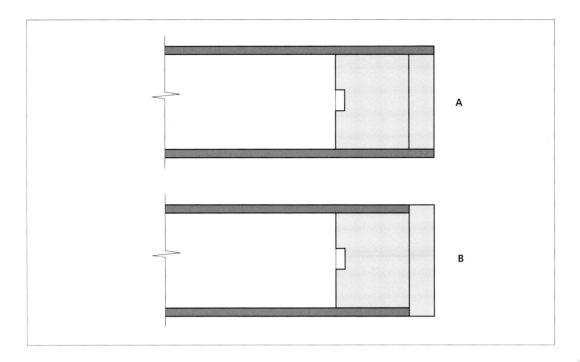

Fig 3.8 **Flush-faced doors. Example A has the lipping concealed by the door face, whereas B has the lipping exposed.**

considering changing both the door and frame, such doors are an extremely good investment as many are also fitted with a series of internal locks on all four sides of the door, operated by a single key. These units are expensive, but extremely secure if fitted properly. If you decide on this option, have the new door fitted by a trained professional to ensure the security you have paid for is not lost as a result of poor fitting.

Security shutters

Roller shutters have been used extensively for many years as security for industrial premises, but more recently they have become more and more popular on the domestic front. You can purchase slimline security shutters for doors and windows at a very reasonable price, and they are an extremely effective deterrent, especially if you are going away for a long period of time. They are available in various colours, designed to harmonize as far as possible with the colour scheme of your house.

Securing internal doors

Most internal doors are of a lighter construction than external doors. 'Flush-faced' doors are faced with either hardboard or plywood, both of which are suitable for painting or applying a wood-patterned veneer for a more natural finish. Some of the more expensive flush-faced doors are finished with a genuine timber veneer, and may also have a hardwood edge known as a 'lipping'. This is frequently concealed by the face veneer (see Fig 3.8).

The internal construction of flush doors also influences their level of security. There are various types of 'core' available. The thickness of flush doors ranges from 35mm (1⅜in) to 54mm (2⅛in), but the majority are between 35mm (1⅜in) for a standard internal door, and 44mm (1¾in) for a fireshield door. Generally the thinner the door the less substantial the interior core, and hence the more vulnerable the door.

Light-framed, hollow core internal flush doors

These are light in weight, being constructed from a light perimeter frame with a very light paper honeycomb lattice core (see Fig 3.9). This light construction means that such doors are fitted with a central block of timber to which the door furniture is affixed. This is known as a 'lock block' (see Fig 3.9). These doors have limited security value, but a well-fitted lock will at least slow down an intruder, and they would need to make a substantial amount of noise to open the door.

The first thing to consider is the hinges. A hollow-core internal door only requires two hinges, but you can upgrade these (see Chapter 4). If the door is held shut by a standard latch with no means of locking, you could consider fitting deadbolts, and this procedure is described later in this chapter, on page 46. Because the door is hollow, you will find that the narrow perimeter frame provides no fixing support for the keyhole plate. If you need to glue the keyhole plates to the face of the door instead of using the screws provided, make sure the plate is in the correct position by sliding it over the key and placing the key in the lock. When it is in place, turn the plate to the upright (horizontal) position and press it into place. If you use superglue, don't stick your finger to the door!

The only occasion where it is necessary to glue the keyhole plate rather than screwing it in place, is when the position of the keyhole falls within the hollow core, as can sometimes be the case when a deadbolt is fitted to a light-framed flush door.

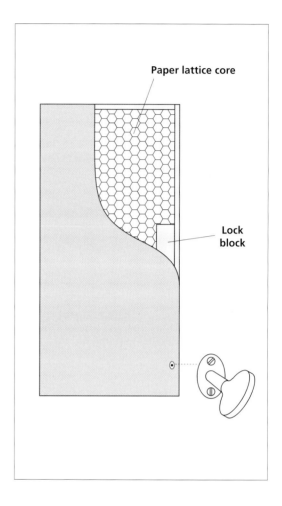

Paper lattice core

Lock block

Fig 3.9 **A light-framed, hollow core, internal flush door with deadbolt.**

Medium-duty internal flush doors

These have a more substantial perimeter frame and a lock rail running the full width of the door (see Fig 3.10). The areas above and below the lock rail are filled with a light, honeycomb lattice paper. Such doors will take most locks and the related door furniture without problems, as the perimeter frames are wide enough to hold the fixing screws. (If you look at

44

the top of the door you will be able to see how wide the stiles are.)

These doors can also be fitted with upper and lower deadbolts and the related keyhole plates in the normal way, using the screws provided. It is not necessary to fit a third hinge to these doors but you must still consider the type of hinges used in line with the recommendations made in Chapter 4.

Solid timber doors

These are heavy-duty doors, 44mm (1¾in) thick. They can be fitted with any type of security lock you feel is required for the location, and also give good sound insulation. Such doors are also 'time rated' for fire resistance properties, according to the manufacturer's specification. However, if such a door is to be used as a fire door, the depth of the frame rebate must be increased in line with fire regulations.

Because of their weight, solid doors require a third hinge, and details of how to fit this appear in Chapter 4, on page 51.

Note

Never fit a lock to a fire escape door, or to any door on route to a fire escape, which cannot be opened easily in a panic situation. There are many such fittings available and I recommend a visit to your local ironmongery stockist if you have any concerns in this regard.

Solid, panelled doors with a compound core

Like solid wooden doors, most doors with a compound core allow you to fit security accessories to any part of the door. However, you may find that some of the materials used for the core have a dusty or foamlike composition, which prevents screws from achieving a

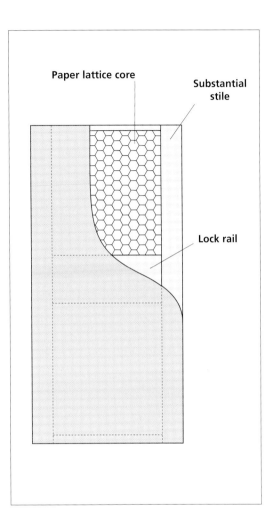

Fig 3.10 Medium-duty internal flush door.

satisfactory purchase. If this is the case, drill a slightly larger hole to take a suitably-sized rawl plug, and refit the screws. The lack of holding power of the core material will not affect any screws holding the lock face in place as these are fitted into the door stile which is normally made from 90mm (3½in) timber.

The thickness of door you choose depends on the security and fire-resistant properties required. They are available up to 54mm (2⅛in) thick, offering an hour of fire resistance, but this would normally be considered too heavy-duty for domestic purposes.

45

Fig 3.11 **Deadbolts and their fixing accessories.**

Fitting deadbolts

Deadbolts (see Fig 3.11) are a valuable addition to door security and are very easy to fit. I recommend that you fit two bolts to each door, 150mm (6in) from the top and the bottom. Measure the width of the bolt's faceplate and be sure not to exceed this when selecting an auger to drill the hole for the bolt. Measure and mark the hole positions dead-centre in the edge of the door.

Select a suitably-sized auger, hold it alongside the bolt, and wrap a piece of insulating tape around the auger as a depth gauge (see Fig 3.12). Place the auger tip on your mark and carefully cut the hole, making sure that you maintain a straight line. Place the bolt into the hole and turn the faceplate until it is parallel with the edge of the door. Use a sharp pencil to mark round the perimeter of the faceplate. Remove the bolt and measure the thickness of the faceplate in order to gauge the depth required so that it finishes flush with the face of the door. Use a

Fig 3.12 **Measure the bolt against the auger and mark the auger with masking tape as a depth gauge. This is an extremely useful and fool-proof method used extensively throughout this book to ensure accurately-drilled receiver holes.**

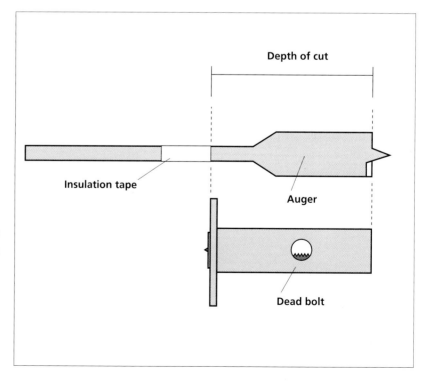

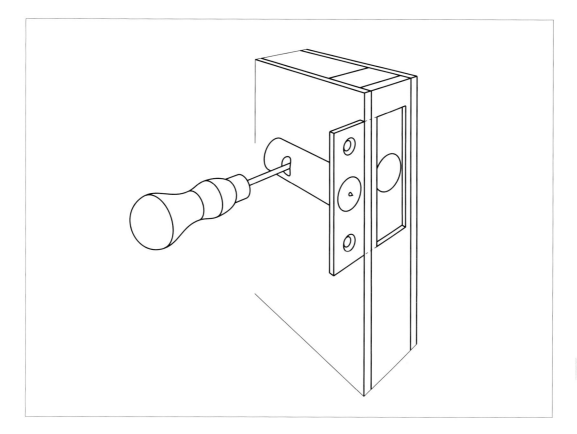

sharp chisel to remove the timber within the perimeter pencil lines to the required depth, but don't try the bolt in place at this stage as you may find it difficult to get out. Hold the deadbolt against the edge of the door on the side you wish to operate the lock, and in line with the cut (see Fig 3.13). Use a bradawl to mark the key access hole and drill it out with a 9mm (⅜in) drill bit on one side of the door only. Once you have cut the key access hole, you can try the bolt in the hole to check the depth of the faceplate recess so that it finishes flush with the door edge. If you need to remove more timber, remove the bolt by putting the key in position and sliding the faceplate clear of its recess. The key access hole is covered by a small plate which is best positioned by sliding it onto the key and fitting the key into the bolt. If you have difficulty getting a good fix for the keyplate screws, refer to page 44 for assistance.

Fig 3.13 Mark the key position by holding the bolt against the appropriate side of the door.

Fitting hinge bolts

Hinge bolts have no moving parts (see Fig 3.14), require no key, are very inexpensive, and are a valuable security aid, particularly on outward-opening doors. The bolts should be fitted close to the hinges, with the fixed pin fitted to the door, and the receiver plate to the rebate of the door frame. The more substantial bolts have a taper on the leading edge to assist in locating the bolt into the receiver. The bolt is fitted in the centre of the door edge, and care needs to be taken when positioning the receiver plate into the frame as there is very little tolerance for smooth operation

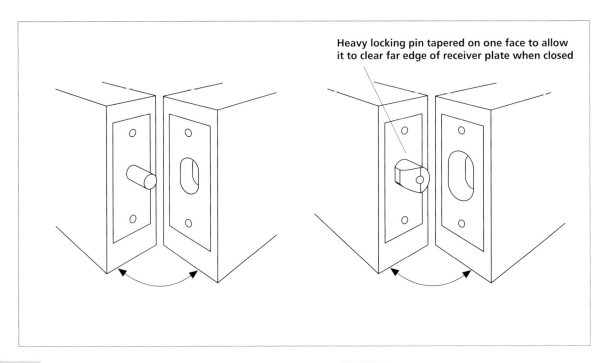

Heavy locking pin tapered on one face to allow it to clear far edge of receiver plate when closed

Fig 3.14 Hinge bolts; light-duty on the left and heavy-duty on the right.

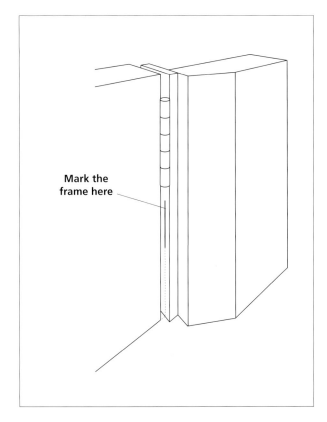

Mark the frame here

of the bolt. Before you start, close the door and see if its back edge is flush with the frame or set into it a little (see Fig 3.15). If the latter is the case, mark the frame in line with the face of the door. Drill a hole for the bolt and fit it into the door, making sure that the sloping face of the bolt is facing the right way to close the door.

Once you have fitted the bolt into the door, measure accurately the distance from the back edge of the bolt to the edge of the door (see Fig 3.16). Transfer this figure to the frame, starting from your original pencil mark which represents the true position of the door face (see Fig 3.17).

Fig 3.15 Check to see if the edge of the door is flush with the frame or set into it a little. If the frame is proud of the face of the door, mark the frame as shown.

Fig 3.16 **Measure distance A.**

Hold the receiver plate in position with the pencil mark just inside the hole in the plate. Make sure the plate is parallel with the edge of the frame, and mark the perimeter of the plate onto the frame. The inner pencil mark indicates the edge of the hole for the receiver pocket. Select an auger as close as possible to the width of the bolt, and cut a pocket in the frame deep enough to receive the length of the bolt. Cut out the timber within the perimeter line to the required depth, to allow the receiver plate to finish flush with the surface of the frame, and fix the receiver plate into position.

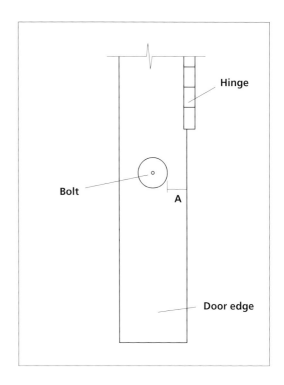

Fig 3.17 **Positioning the rebate bolt receiver.**

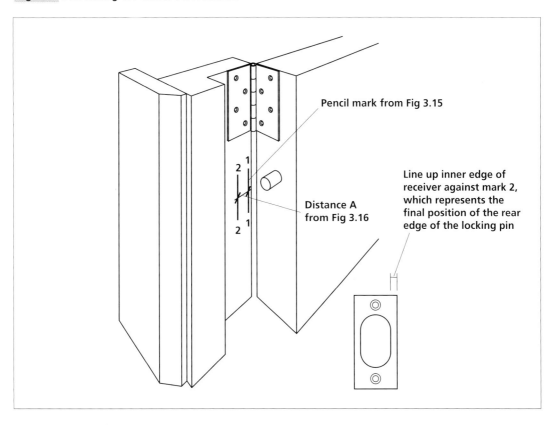

4 Upgrading hinges

As I have already mentioned, hinges are an important element of security. There is a wide variety of hinges on the market for numerous purposes, and what follows is a general review of the commonly-used types and the level of security they afford. Remember, on any door that opens outwards, the knuckle of the hinge will be exposed, making it easy to remove the pin, and you should fit hinge bolts. The procedure for this is fully described in Chapter 3, on page 47.

Types of hinge

Pressed-steel butt hinges

These are for internal use, and will deteriorate if exposed to the elements. Some pressed steel hinges have a removable pin in the knuckle holding the two leaves together (see Fig 4.1). This pin is still accessible when the door is closed and can easily be removed by tapping the end of the pin with a nail punch and pulling it out with a pair of pliers. The door can then be opened from the hinge side. Such hinges should be replaced with either a fixed-pin, pressed-steel butt hinge or a pressed-steel hinge with interlocking security lugs. These are pressed out of the hinge leaf and lock both leaves of the hinge together when the door is

Fig 4.1 Pressed-steel butt hinge. The pin holding such hinges together is very easy to remove.

closed (refer to Fig 1.1 on page 4). Another option is to fit hinge bolts, as detailed in Chapter 3.

Brass butt hinges

Not to be confused with the thin, brass-plated steel butts used on internal doors. These hinges are suitable for external use and are most commonly used on front entrance doors. Good-quality brass hinges will have stainless steel washers fitted between the fingers of the knuckle so as to reduce wear. Although these hinges are not vulnerable in themselves, it is always a good idea to fit hinge bolts as detailed in Chapter 3.

Cast-iron hinges

These are most suited to outdoor positions (cast iron does not rust). They are commonly found in rear entrance doors, because, while less expensive than brass hinges, they are not very attractive to look at. If these hinges are fitted to an outward-opening door it is very important to fit hinge bolts because cast iron is very brittle and the hinge can be completely shattered with a single blow from a hammer.

Fitting a third hinge

External door hinges are designed to carry the weight of a heavy door but it is wise to fit all external doors with a third hinge, so that they have 'one and a half pairs'.

Begin by opening the door as wide as possible and deciding the height of the new hinge. This should be in the middle of the door edge or slightly above. Middle hinges are often fitted above-centre, as this reduces tension on the top hinge during use, because the weight of the

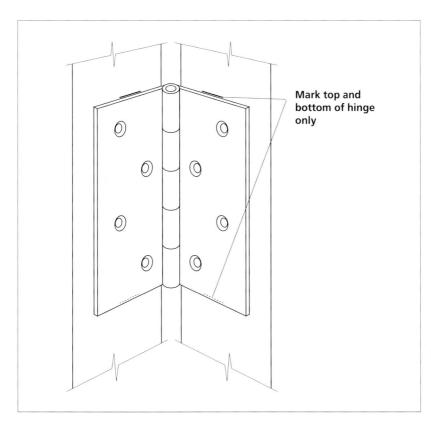

Mark top and bottom of hinge only

Fig 4.2 **Mark the position of the top and bottom of the hinge, but *not* that of the long edge at this stage, because this will change when you set the hinge into the door and the frame.**

Fig 4.3 Make sure the new hinge aligns with the existing hinges.

door effectively pulls the top hinge away from the frame and pushes the bottom hinge into the frame. Next, hold the hinge in position, and use a pencil to mark the position of the top and bottom of the hinge only (see Fig 4.2). Make sure the long edge of the new hinge is in line with the existing hinges, otherwise the smooth operation of the door will be affected, and it may tend to spring open. Such doors are termed as being 'hinge bound'.

To accurately align the new hinge with the existing hinges, place a straight edge against the outer edge of the top and bottom hinge as shown in Fig 4.3. Use a pencil to mark the two vertical edge positions for the new hinge. Measure the thickness of the hinge leaf in order to gauge the depth of cut for the hinge recess. You may notice that the hinge leaf tapers down in thickness from the knuckle to the outer edge. This needs to be taken into account when cutting out the recess.

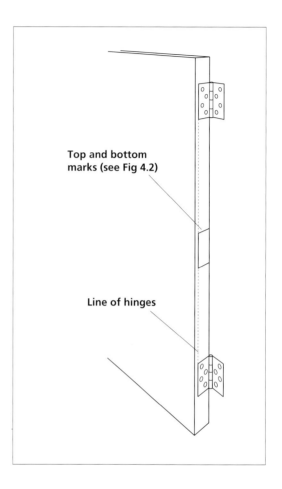

Top and bottom marks (see Fig 4.2)

Line of hinges

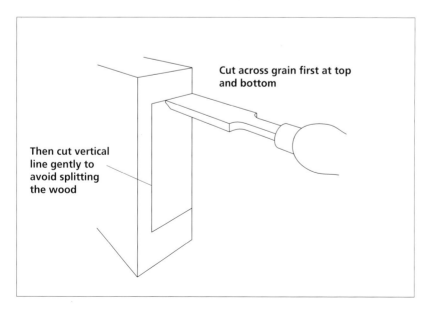

Cut across grain first at top and bottom

Then cut vertical line gently to avoid splitting the wood

Fig 4.4 Cut the rebate for the hinge.

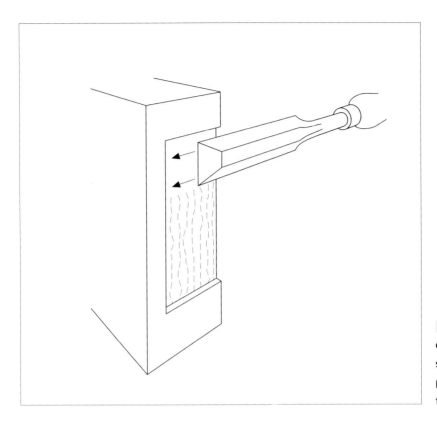

Fig 4.5 **Hold the chisel flat against the surface and gently pare it smooth, ready for the hinge.**

Now cut out the marked area so that the hinge face finishes flush with the door edge. Take care not to go beyond the pencil lines, and don't go too deep as this will put the hinge out of line with the existing hinges.

Use a sharp chisel to cut across the grain first (see Fig 4.4). Continue cutting around the perimeter lines. Take your time; there's no need to reach the final depth on the first cut. When you cut along the length of the recess, the chisel will sink into the timber far more easily, as you are cutting with the grain, so apply a little less pressure.

Once the perimeter line has been cut cleanly, use a broad chisel and a mallet, starting close to the end of the recess and working back to the middle. Cut the perimeter line again and repeat the whole process until you reach the required depth. Smooth off the base of the cut with the flat face of the chisel (see Fig 4.5).

Fig 4.6 **A tee hinge (top) and a band and gudgeon hinge (bottom).**

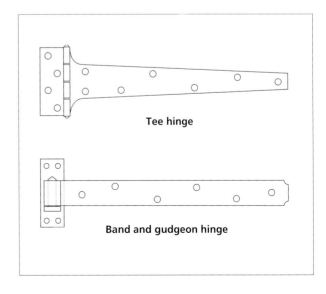

Tee hinge

Band and gudgeon hinge

Tee hinges

Tee hinges are those found on, for example, rear entrance gates, stable doors and garage doors. They are vulnerable to intruders because they have exposed screw heads (see Fig 4.6, and refer back to Figs 1.11 and 1.12 on page 11).

If ordinary straight slot screws have been used then a number of things can be done to improve the security of the hinge.

▼ Remove some or all of the screws and replace them with security screws. If you decide to do this, don't take all the screws out at once, or you will be wrestling with the weight of the door. Take them out two at a time, fitting the new security screws in their place as you go.

▼ Remove the straight slot screws and replace them with cross-head screws. Once you have systematically replaced all the screws, use a power drill with a 9mm (⅜in) high speed drill bit to drill out the cross head just enough so that the screw can no longer be turned. Always use safety goggles when using a power drill.

▼ If you are looking for more substantial security, take out the top and bottom screws from the frame plate, and three screws from the long arm of the hinge. Then drill through the door using a 6mm (¼in) drill bit inserted into the vacant screw positions, and fit 6mm (¼in) galvanized or stainless steel bolts through the holes extending approximately 10mm (⅜in) through the door. Then fit a 25mm (1in) plate washer at the rear of the door (refer to Fig 1.13 on page 12), followed by the bolt nuts. This will stop the nut sinking into the door. Finally, use a ball-pein hammer to tap around the end of the 6mm (¼in) bolt which will prevent the nut from working loose through tampering with the external bolt heads.

Fitting a mortise lock

5

The housing required for a mortise lock can range from a single drilled hole to accommodate a dead bolt, to a series of holes in line to form an elongated mortise, long enough and deep enough to accommodate the body of the lock purchased. The basic principles of fitting are the same.

The following describes how to fit a five-lever mortise sash lock (see Fig 5.1). Before you begin, I recommend that you check the following:

▼ Are the stiles of the door deep enough to accommodate the lock?
▼ Is the lock of the correct hand for closing (see Fig 5.2)?

Fig 5.1 A five-lever mortise sash lock.

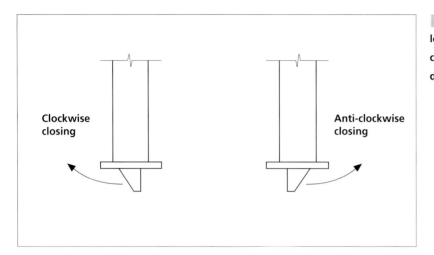

Fig 5.2 Check that the lock you buy is the correct hand for the door concerned.

Clockwise closing

Anti-clockwise closing

If you haven't already read Chapter 3, which includes information on construction, *please* do so. Failure to appreciate standard methods of door construction when fitting locks could result in your unnecessarily weakening the middle rail joints of a glazed or panelled timber-framed door by cutting into the joints, and in the case of internal flush doors could leave you with very limited possibilities to fix any door furniture to the door.

Marking the lock position

Hold the lock in one hand, and offer it up to the leading edge (locking stile) of the door at the intended fixing position. Use a pencil to mark the upper and lower points of the mortise position on the leading edge of the door.

There are three ways to define the mortise centre line which the auger will follow when cutting the hole for the mortise. You can use a marking gauge, *provided* you are confident enough not to go beyond the intended upper and lower stop points, beyond which any gauge marks will not be covered by the face of the lock when the job is complete.

A safer method is to use a combination square and pencil. Set the combination square to what looks like half the width of the leading edge of the door (see Fig 5.3a). Transfer this setting onto the leading edge anywhere in between the upper and lower marks. Turn the unaltered square to the opposite face and repeat the process (see Fig 5.3b). You will now have two marks close to one another from which the centre line can easily be found and checked by readjusting the combination square and repeating the process. Slide the square and pencil between the two points (be careful not to scratch the door), making a centre line which your auger tip will follow (see Fig 5.3c).

If you don't have a combination square, the following very simple method can be used with pinpoint accuracy. Use a piece of card or paper to mark three points 30mm (1¼in) apart, giving a total of 60mm (2⅜in). Note that this distance is *wider* than the door edge. Hold the card against the door edge on a diagonal until the two outer marks are in line with the edge on both sides. The middle mark is the centre line position (see Fig 5.4). Do this at the top and bottom of the lock position, and then join up the two points with a straight edge.

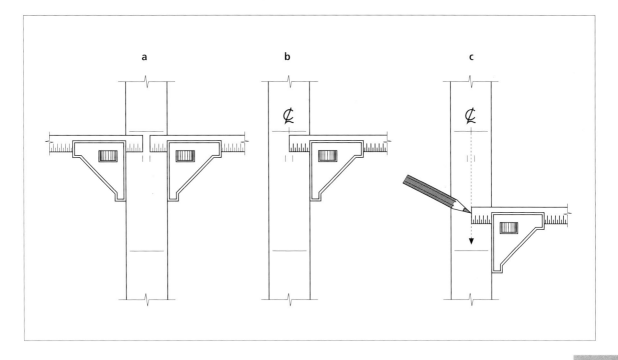

a   b   c

Fig 5.3 Using a combination square to find the centre line.

Fig 5.4 Using a piece of card, marked as shown, to find the centre line.

Choosing the right auger

Most manufacturers indicate the auger size required on the pack. If not, or if you are re-positioning an existing lock, you need to choose the auger size carefully. If the auger is too big it will weaken the door more than necessary, and may even be wider than the faceplate of the lock. Once you have begun the cut it will be too late, so always check the size *before* you begin the cut.

A simple way to determine the auger size is to hold the auger against the body of the lock. Is it a little wider than the lock body but still narrower than the faceplate? If so, it is the correct size for the job. If you are unsure, try it out on a scrap piece of timber.

There is always a risk of cutting too deep and bursting the back of the stile, so it is helpful to be able to gauge the depth of the cut *during* the operation. Use insulation tape to mark the auger at the correct depth of cut (see Fig 5.5).

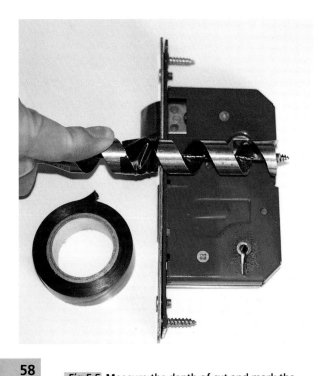

Bracing the door

Before you begin cutting, make sure that the door is held firm by wedging it at its base (see Fig 5.6). The basic principle of an effective wedge is the lower the angle, the more effective it becomes. The higher the angle, the higher will be the risk of the wedge working loose during use. Any door movement while you are fitting the lock could result in a poor finish. You will see that the wedges shown in Fig 5.6 have blunt ends which provide a small but effective striking face which will assist in their removal when the job is complete.

Fig 5.5 Measure the depth of cut and mark the auger with insulating tape, as shown.

Fig 5.6 Wedge the door from both sides.

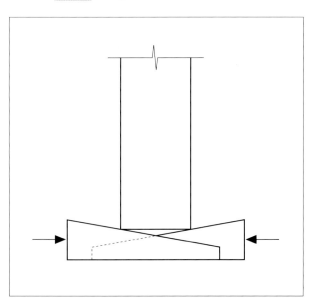

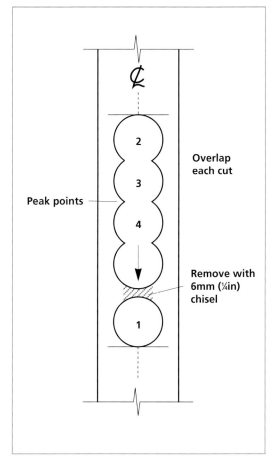

Fig 5.7 Drill overlapping holes in the sequence shown.

Cutting the mortise

Drill *one* hole only, at the base of the mortise position. Make sure you don't go beyond the lower mortise line with the auger. Next, from the top of the mortise, drill more holes working down towards the first hole, overlapping the holes as you go (see Fig 5.7). When you get down to the bottom (first) hole you may end up with a small section of uncut timber which will be difficult to remove with the auger, and should be removed using a 6mm (¼in) chisel and a mallet.

Continuing with the 6mm (¼in) chisel, clean out the loose chippings so that you can see the mortise sides more clearly for paring or dressing the peak points with a sharp, broad chisel. Do *not* blow in the hole when clearing the mortise of chippings, as there is a high risk of eye injury.

Fixing the faceplate

The body of the lock should slide smoothly into the mortise. Remember, if you have difficulty getting the lock in you will certainly have difficulty getting it out, so *never* force it. Once the body of the lock is fully in the mortise, you will notice that you have a small degree of movement. Use one hand to centralize the faceplate on the door edge, with equal distance on both sides, making sure at the same time that it is parallel with the door edge along its length. Mark around the perimeter of the faceplate, and then cut the wood to the required depth (i.e. the thickness of the plate). Always keep *within* the lines with your chisel, and remember that a chisel will travel slightly *away* from its bevel angle when it is struck unless it is held firmly.

When cutting the recess for the faceplate, it is best to remove the wood directly above and below the mortise first, and then work gently toward the outer edges of the door (see Fig 5.8). This will reduce the risk of splitting the door edge as you get near it. If you have cut the recess

successfully, the pencil lines marking the outline should still be visible when you have finished.

To check your progress, turn the lock around, hold the body and enter *only* the faceplate into the recess, removing it gently to protect the end grain from being pulled away with the lock (see Fig 5.9).

Spindle and key positions

Place the lock at the side of the door, holding it in line with the faceplate recess, and flush with the edge of the door. With the lock held firm, mark the centre of the spindle position and the *upper*

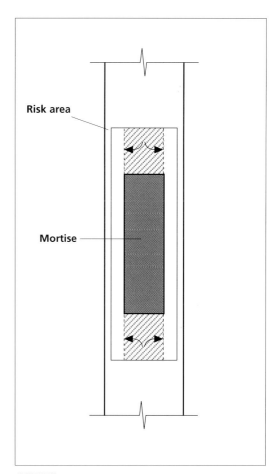

Risk area

Mortise

Fig 5.8 **Remove the shaded area first, then gently work to the left and right.**

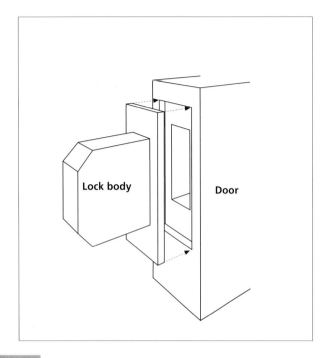

circular part of the key position by inserting a bradawl through the holes in the side of the lock, pressing firmly to give a centre point for cutting these positions. Repeat the process on the opposite face of the door (see Fig 5.10).

To cut the spindle position, use a 16mm (⅝in) bit. Cut only *halfway* through the door, *not* through to the opposite face, as this may result in damage to the door. Repeat the operation from the opposite side. To cut the key position, use a 10mm (⅜in) bit and repeat the spindle positioning process. The 10mm (⅜in) hole does not make any allowance for the fingers of the key to pass through the door into the lock, so the wood beneath the hole needs to be elongated by gentle use of a 6mm (¼in)

Fig 5.9 Check your progress by inserting the faceplate only.

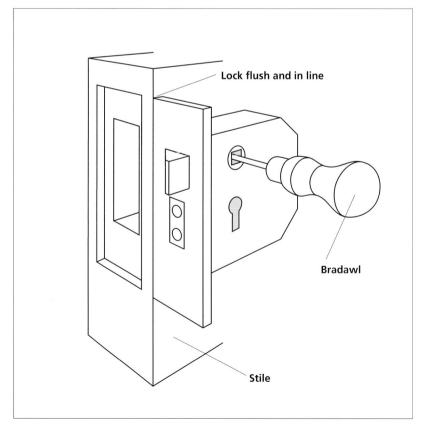

Fig 5.10 Hold the lock flush with the door edge and in line with the faceplate recess, and mark the spindle and key hole positions on the door.

chisel, just enough to allow uninterrupted passage of the key into the lock from both sides.

Depending on the make of lock, you may have to remove the faceplate in order to expose the fixing points for the lock. Once you have secured the lock and secured the faceplate, check that the plate is flush with the door, and that the spindle and key positions of the lock line up with the holes you have cut for them.

Door furniture

First, slide the spindle through the door and fit the furniture onto the spindle on both sides. Make sure you have put the handles on the correct sides, as they are handed. Check also that the spindle is the required length, and shorten it with a hacksaw if necessary (make sure not to cut it too short!).

There will be a large degree of pivotal movement of the furniture, the centre point being the spindle. This needs to be stabilized so as to fit the furniture in line with the door edge, as with the lock faceplate.

Once you are happy with the position of the furniture, use a bradawl to penetrate two of the four fixing points, one at the top and one diagonally at the bottom. Let go, and examine the result. Is it lined up with the door edge? If not, you will still have a little horizontal flexibility without removing the screws, but if it needs more than a gentle tap, remove the screws and try again. Do *not* force the furniture against the spindle, as this will damage the components and lead to poor operation of the latch and lock. Once you are satisfied, you can put in the remaining screws and try the handle for smooth operation.

Reversing the closing hand

If you are transferring an existing lock to an alternative location, it is always possible that the latch is facing in the wrong direction for closing.

However, it is a relatively simple procedure to turn the latch around.

With some locks, you can remove one small screw on the side of the lock body, drawing the latch forward, turning it to face the opposite direction and returning the screw to its place. In the majority of cases, however, you will need to open the lock body to get at the parts requiring turning.

Before you start, please read *all* the following because you will spend less time reading this than you will spend looking for springs that have gone to explore your carpet or workshop floor!

The procedure is as follows:

1 Place the lock on a clean flat surface, with the side screws uppermost. Remove the screws holding the two sides of the body together, and put them safely out of the way.

2 Put your finger on the spindle port so as to stabilize it whilst separating the two sides (see Fig 5.11).

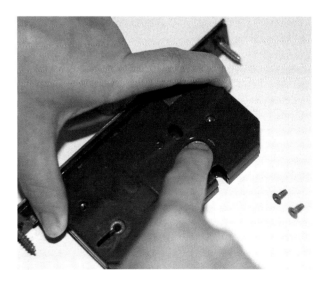

Fig 5.11 **Put your finger on the spindle port while you separate the two sides of the lock.**

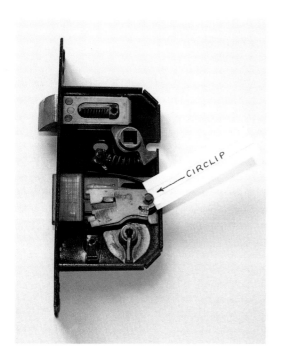

Fig 5.12 (left) See if the bolt lever components are held in place by a circlip.

Fig 5.13 (below) Use a screwdriver to gently remove the springs.

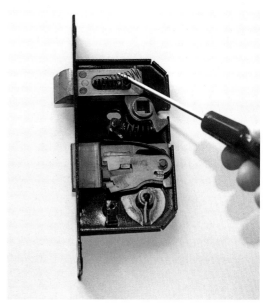

3 Once the side has been removed *don't* move the lock. Look carefully at the lever components that would operate the bolt to see if these are held in place by a small circlip – in which case you can breathe again (see Fig 5.12) – or if they are free to spring out in every direction at the slightest provocation. If they are not restrained you will need to place your finger over them whilst the other hand turns the latch.

4 Look at the simple operation of the latch. It is not difficult to remove the springs but take care not to lose them. It is best to put a small screwdriver right through the springs and draw it back gently to remove them (see Fig 5.13). You can now turn the latch over and reverse the procedure to rebuild the lock (see Fig 5.14).

Fig 5.14 Reverse the latch and then replace the springs.

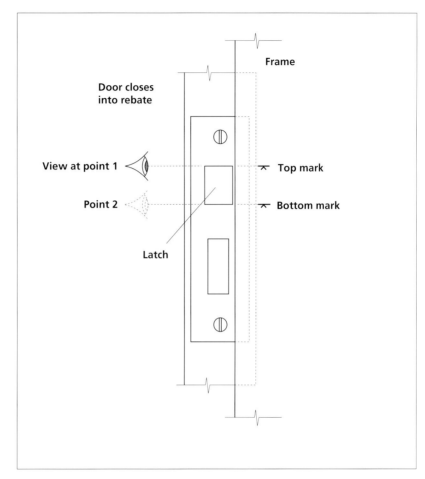

Fig 5.15 Mark the frame in line with the top and bottom of the latch.

Frame

Door closes into rebate

View at point 1

Point 2

Latch

Top mark

Bottom mark

63

When you remove your finger from the lock components, the top lever will tend to stick to your finger, so remove it carefully. Once rebuilt, you would have to have an extremely strong disposition to resist trying both the latch and bolt for smooth operation so once you have finished playing with it you can fit it to the door.

Fitting the receiver plate

A receiver plate is fitted to the door frame, precisely opposite the lock, to receive the latch and bolt when closing and securing the door. There are two types of receiver plate. A plate with two holes to receive the latch and bolt, or a plate with a steel box attached to the rear for added security.

Basic plate

To fit a basic receiver plate, follow this procedure:

1 Bend down so that you can see the precise point where the latch will strike the frame. Use a pencil to mark the frame at the top and bottom positions of the latch (see Fig 5.15).

2 Open the door and rub the side of your pencil along the outer edge of the latch, giving it a good coat of pencil lead. Use the furniture to

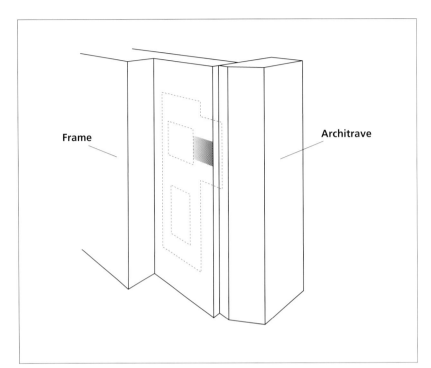

Frame

Architrave

Fig 5.16 **The leaded latch will mark the area of the frame clearly, between the two pencil marks you have already made.**

draw back the latch and close the door into the rebate. Release the furniture, allowing the latch to rub against the frame, and gently open and close the door so as to allow the pencil lead to mark the latch position in the frame rebate.

3 Open the door fully. You should now have a distinct mark where the latch came into contact with the door frame rebate (see Fig 5.16).

4 Look closely at Fig 5.16 in order to correctly position the receiver plate over the mark made by the latch. Make sure the plate is parallel with the frame, and draw around the perimeter with a sharp pencil, keeping the pencil tight to the edge. The plate is not very thick so don't go too deep when setting it in, and remember the principle of leaving the line on. You will see that you have to go a little deeper on the leading edge of the plate where the latch will strike.

5 Once you have a good fit you can fix the plate. Use a bradawl with a chisel point to break the grain prior to fitting any screws. (A spike point will separate the grain, resulting in splitting which could extend beyond the plate edge.) If you don't have a chisel-point bradawl, place a nail point upward with its head resting on a solid surface, and tap the point lightly so as to flatten it a little. This will be just as good. If you find yourself without a drill bit for pilot holes, a nail rested on its side and the tip flattened to a diamond shape, although not as strong, will prove a good alternative.

6 With the receiver plate fixed in position, cut the recesses for the latch and lock using a 6mm (¼in) chisel, working from the middle out, but *gently* so as not to damage the faceplate. Carrying out this activity whilst the plate is fitted will remove the need to mark the positions out, and help keep the sides of the openings square and true.

Fig 5.17 **Position the faceplate over the latch and mark the rebate as shown.**

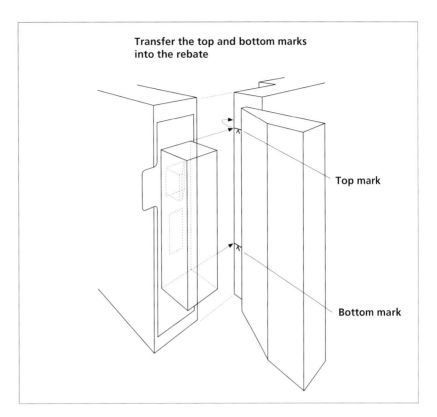

Transfer the top and bottom marks into the rebate

Top mark

Bottom mark

You can easily assess the required depth by turning the key and measuring the bolt length.

Security plate

1 First mark the top and bottom of the box on the door frame. Open the door and face the lock. Place the box receiver over the lock, in the position it will eventually take. Gently close the door until the back of the box is touching the frame, and mark the upper and lower positions. Transfer these marks to the rebate (see Fig 5.17).

2 With the box receiver still in place, measure the distance from the inner edge of the box to the closing edge of the door. Add 0.5mm and transfer this measurement to the intended position in the frame rebate (see Fig 5.18). You now have the inner line (side 1), for the box recess. Next measure

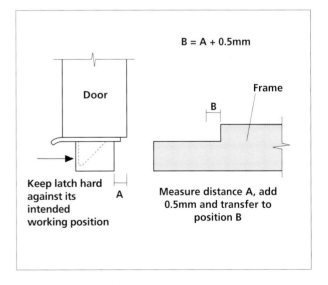

B = A + 0.5mm

Door

Frame

B

Keep latch hard against its intended working position

A

Measure distance A, add 0.5mm and transfer to position B

Fig 5.18 **Measure the distance from the inner edge of the box to the edge of the door as shown. Add 0.5mm and transfer this measurement to the frame rebate.**

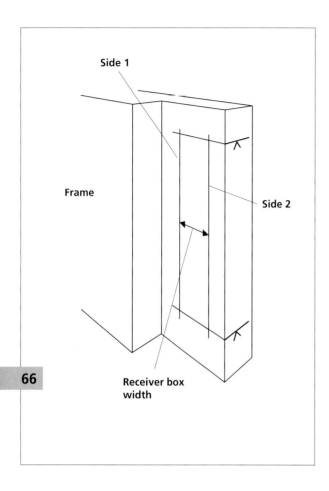

Side 1

Frame

Side 2

Receiver box
width

Fig 5.19 Measure the width of the box and mark the outer line (side 2).

the width of the box, and mark side 2 (see Fig 5.19). You now have the position for the back box recess. Measure the required depth, and cut the recess by drilling a series of holes with a suitably-sized auger and cleaning out with a sharp chisel.

3 You now need to locate the perimeter line of the faceplate. Put the back box into the recess so that the rear of the faceplate is hard against the frame. This is a good opportunity to check the latch operating position. You might have enough space between the door and the frame when the door is closed to fix the faceplate back to the surface of the frame without setting it in. This will allow you to check the operation of the lock at this stage by closing the door. If all is well, mark the position of the faceplate and set it into the frame. If there is insufficient space to carry out this test, you will need to check the final position by measuring the distance from the flat face of the latch to the rear edge of the door and compare this with the distance from the back of the rebate to the working edge of the faceplate (see Fig 5.20). If the measurements indicate that the latch will operate effectively and the faceplate is parallel, mark the perimeter of the faceplate and set it in. Now try the door for closing and turn the key to check the lock works smoothly. Feels good, doesn't it!

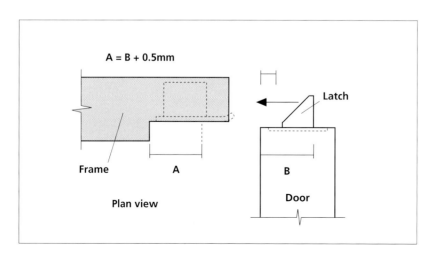

A = B + 0.5mm

Frame

A

Plan view

Latch

B

Door

Fig 5.20 Confirming the required operating position for the receiver box.

Tower and flush bolts

6

Tower bolts

Tower bolts are the simplest form of security lock. The basic design is very strong and provides a good level of security (as long as access to the sliding bolt is denied!). There are a variety of designs available for different purposes.

The basic steel tower bolt, shown in Fig 6.1, is commonly used to secure back garden gates, but they are also available in brass and aluminium for general use around the home. Smaller tower bolts offer little in the way of security, as any 'surface fixed lock' (such as a bolt) is only as strong as the screws holding the receiver in place.

Fitting a tower bolt

To fit a tower bolt and ensure smooth operation, hold it level against the door in the required position and mark one of the upper screw positions through the holes in the back plate (see Fig 6.1). Hold a piece of card with a square corner against the door edge as shown in Fig 6.1, and line up the top edge of the bolt with the horizontal edge of the card. You can now mark a second screw position through the back plate, and use a bradawl to pierce a pilot hole for the second fixing screw. Fit the remainder of the fixing screws in the same manner. Now turn your attention to the slide bolt receiver.

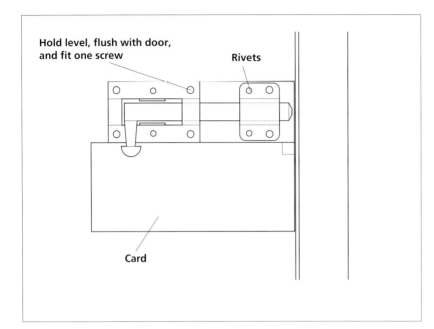

Hold level, flush with door, and fit one screw

Rivets

Card

Fig 6.1 A basic tower bolt. Hold a piece of card against the bottom of the tower bolt to help you square it up.

Fig 6.2 Position the receiver centrally over the bolt and make pilot holes for the screws with a bradawl.

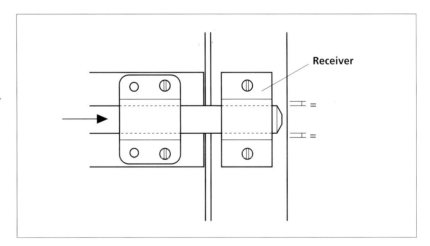

Receiver

First, close the gate into the frame and slide the bolt. If the bolt slides smoothly across the face of the frame without catching, you have an easy job; simply position the receiver centrally over the bolt. Use a bradawl to mark the two fixing points and fit the screws (see Fig 6.2).

If when you first close the gate you find that the bolt will not slide due to hitting the door frame, you will need to set the receiver into the frame so that the bolt will slide smoothly into it. Close the gate and mark the frame in line with the plate of the bolt (see Fig 6.3). Now open the gate a little to allow the bolt to slide across the front of the frame. Hold the receiver in position over the slide bolt, making sure it is central and flush with the edge of the frame (see Fig 6.4). Use a pencil to mark around the perimeter of the receiver and join up your marks to show the area of wood that needs to be removed.

Now cut out the timber with a sharp chisel and a mallet, but take care not to go beyond any of the pencil marks. First cut into the top and bottom marks going across the grain. You don't need to go all the way in as this would make it more difficult to control the chisel. Gently tap the chisel just a couple of millimetres or so into the timber so as to clearly define the perimeter line, and clean out the area down to the depth of the line (see Fig 6.5). Continue the process until you have a level base to fit the bolt receiver. Hold the receiver in position hard against the back of the

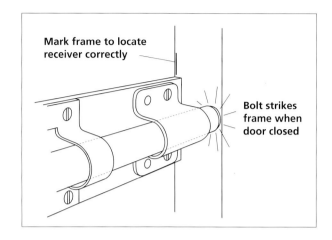

Mark frame to locate receiver correctly

Bolt strikes frame when door closed

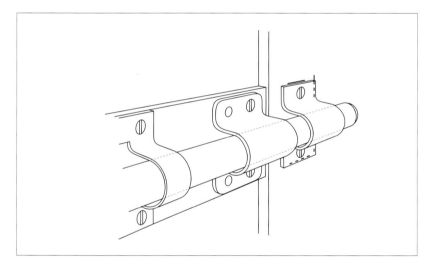

Fig 6.3 (above) Close the gate and mark the frame in line with the plate of the bolt.

Fig 6.4 (middle) Mark the perimeter of the receiver on the frame.

69

Fig 6.5 (below) Clean down to the required depth using your marks as a guide.

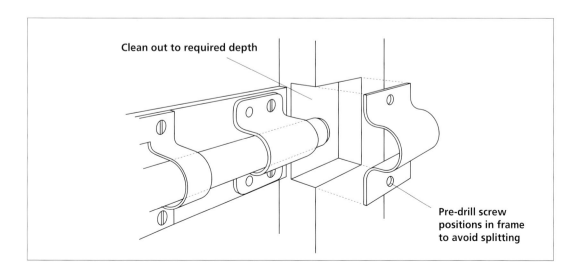

Clean out to required depth

Pre-drill screw positions in frame to avoid splitting

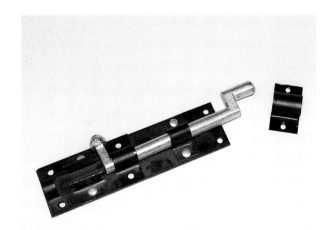

Fig 6.6 A cranked tower bolt.

recess and try the bolt for smooth operation. If the bolt enters the receiver without a problem but hits the frame and doesn't locate into its lockdown slot, you may need to deepen the recess a little.

Great care needs to be taken when fitting the screws holding the receiver. If you split the frame you will reduce the strength of the lock. If you use a bradawl to pilot the screw holes make sure it has a chisel point which will break the grain of the timber and not separate the grain resulting in the wood splitting. If you are using a drill bit to make the pilot screw holes make sure it is of the correct size.

Cranked tower bolts

These are used when the bolt needs to slide into a solid frame, and are designed to keep the bolt away from the frame rebate (see Figs 6.6 and 6.7).

Fig 6.7 (below) Tower bolts are used when the bolt needs to slide into a solid frame. The bolt position is found by closing the door and marking the position where the end of the bolt touches the frame. Set the bolt just a little bit back from the frame so that it won't catch when you close the door.

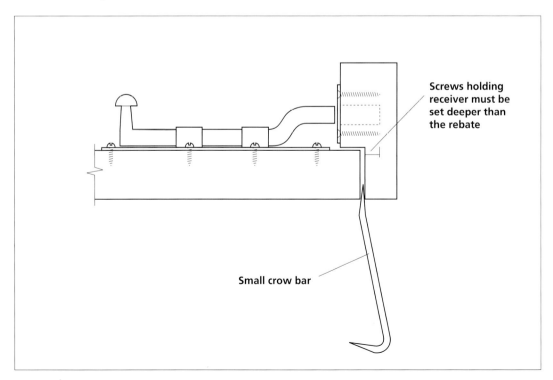

Screws holding receiver must be set deeper than the rebate

Small crow bar

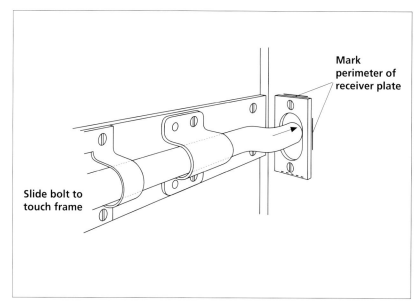

Fig 6.8 To position the receiver plate, slide the bolt so that it touches the frame through the receiver plate's hole, and mark around the perimeter of the plate, ensuring the plate is squared up.

Mark perimeter of receiver plate

Slide bolt to touch frame

71

Fitting a cranked bolt is the same as fitting a straight tower bolt, except that the end of the bolt is not in line with the door edge. Fit the bolt just clear of the frame so that it does not catch the frame when the door is opened. The receiver for this type of bolt is a flat plate with a centre hole to receive the bolt.

Cranked tower bolts have the advantage of greater resistance to forced entry because the screws of the receiver plate are under shear stress from the side when the door is pushed. However, the rebate is not far away and will split when pressure is applied from the side with, say, a small crow bar. If you wish to reduce the risk of forced entry, increase the length of the screws beyond the rebate depth as shown in Fig 6.7.

After fitting the cranked bolt, hold the receiver plate in position and slide the bolt until it touches the solid frame. Mark round the perimeter of the receiver plate (see Fig 6.8). Use a drill bit which is slightly larger than the width of the bolt to drill a hole in the marked position on the frame, which will allow the bolt to slide its full length, and try the bolt for smooth operation. Mark the screw positions, pilot the screw holes with either a bradawl or drill and fit the screws. If you feel that the receiver plate would look better if it was finished flush with the frame face, simply mark the perimeter of the plate while it is in place, remove it and gently cut away the required depth of timber with a sharp chisel.

Push bolts for wooden-framed doors

If you are looking for a more attractive alternative to the standard tower bolt, a push bolt, as shown in Fig 6.9, may be the answer. These have concealed fixing screws and a sturdy 9mm (⅜in) sliding bolt. They are operated by pushing the slide bolt into the receiver, as with a standard tower bolt, but they can only be unlocked by using a key to release the spring mechanism. The bolts come with two types of receiver plate to suit either face of the door.

Fig 6.9 A push bolt.

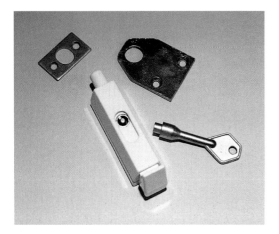

Fig 6.10 Use the key to release the bolt.

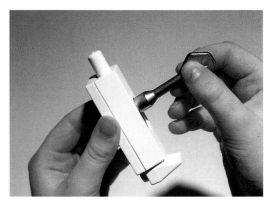

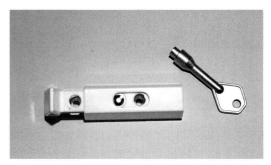

Fig 6.11 You will now be able to see the two holes through which the fixing screws will pass.

Fitting push bolts

You can fit push bolts either to the 'opening side' or to the 'frame side' of a door. To fit a bolt to the 'opening side', hold the bolt in one hand and use the key to release the spring-loaded bolt, as shown in Fig 6.10. You will now be able to see two holes in the front face of the lock where the fixing screws will pass through (see Fig 6.11). Hold the lock in the chosen position, close to the edge

72

Fig 6.12 Hold the bolt in the desired position close to the top of the door and mark the screw positions with a bradawl.

of the door, and use a bradawl to mark the screw positions (see Fig 6.12). Secure the push bolt to the door with two of the larger screws and then slide the bolt into the locked position. Use the larger of the two receiver plates, which is designed to be fixed into the head of the door frame rebate on the opening side, and protrude forward to allow the bolt to enter the receiver (see Fig 6.13).

Depending upon the clearance between the top of the door and the door frame, you may need to set the receiver plate into the frame to avoid it catching. Mark the centre line of the plate, by marking the centre line of the bolt onto the edge of the frame (see Fig 6.14 a and b). There are three ways to ensure the receiver plate is positioned accurately.

1 Open the door and place the plate over the bolt, as shown in Fig 6.15. Close the door, allowing the plate to slide between the door and the frame. If the door won't close due to the thickness of the plate, try method 2,

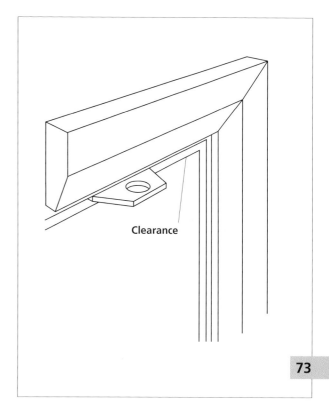

Clearance

73

Fig 6.13 Use the larger of the two receiver plates supplied with the bolt if you are fitting the bolt to the 'opening side' of the door.

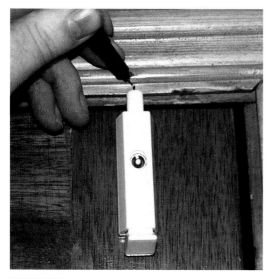

Fig 6.14a

Fig 6.14b

Mark the centre line of the bolt onto the frame as a guide for positioning the receiver plate.

Fig 6.15 (above) Open the door and place the plate over the bolt.

Fig 6.16 (top right) Make sure the bolt is close to but not touching the front of the hole in the receiver plate.

Fig 6.17 (below) Measure the distance from the back of the receiver plate to the back of the rebate.

overleaf. If the door closes, check that the front of the receiver is parallel with the face of the push lock, and that the bolt is close to, but not touching, the front of the hole in the receiver (see Fig 6.16). Use a pencil or felt-tip pen to mark the midway position where the receiver meets the frame, as shown in Fig 6.17. Open the door and remove the plate from the bolt. Hold the plate in position with the midway pencil mark in line with the edge

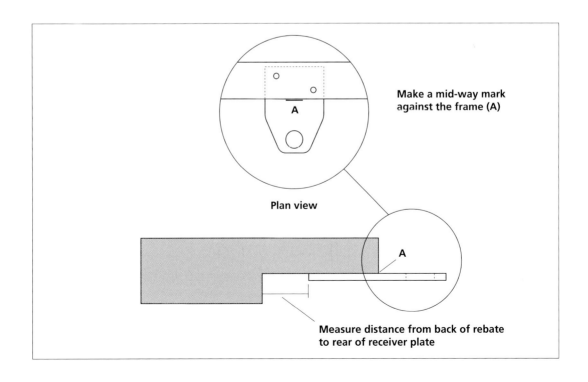

Make a mid-way mark against the frame (A)

A

Plan view

A

Measure distance from back of rebate to rear of receiver plate

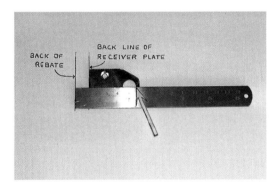

Fig 6.19 Mark the distance measured in Fig 6.18 on to a piece of card to show the distance from the back of the rebate to the rear of the receiver plate.

Fig 6.20 Mark the position of the front face of the slide bolt.

Fig 6.18 Make a note of the distance between the back of the rebate and the front of the bolt, and add 1mm.

of the frame (see Fig 6.17). Measure the distance from the back end of the plate to the back of the rebate, and draw a parallel line on the frame for the rear of the receiver plate to follow (see Fig 6.17). Now hold the plate in position with the bolt centre line visible through the hole in the plate. Mark the screw positions with a bradawl and fix the plate in position. Try the lock for smooth operation and if all is well, remove the timber behind the plate to set it in flush with the frame.

2 Once you have fitted the bolt to the door, close the door and slide a steel rule between the bolt and the top of the door frame. Make a note of the distance from the back of the rebate to the front of the bolt (see Fig 6.18), and add 1mm. Hold the steel rule against the face of the receiver plate, with the measurement in line with the front of the large hole, as shown in Fig 6.19. Now read the measurement on the rule at the back of the plate. This will give you the distance from the back of the rebate to the back of the receiver plate, allowing you to mark a line on the frame for the back of the plate to follow (see Fig 6.17).

3 Equally good results can be achieved using a piece of card instead of a steel rule. Close the door and slide a piece of card over the top of the door in line with the bolt. Make sure that the card goes right to the back of the rebate, mark the position of the front face of the slide bolt (see Fig 6.20) and the front face of the door rebate (see Fig 6.21). Remove the

75

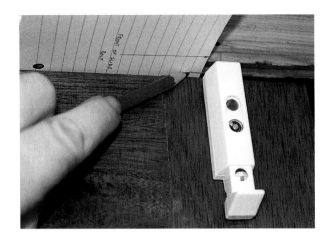

Fig 6.21 (left) Then mark the position of the front face of the door rebate.

Fig 6.22 (below) Mark the rear of the plate on the card, as shown.

card, hold it against the receiver plate with the pencil mark just inside the bolt hole and mark the position of the back of the plate on the card (see Fig 6.22). Hold the card in position on the frame, and using the second pencil mark as a guide, draw a line to position the rear of the plate (see Fig 6.23).

If you need to fit a push bolt to the frame side of a door, remember that you cannot fit the bolt to the perimeter of the door, as this will be covered by the rebate (see Fig 6.24). To determine the correct position for the bolt, close the door and hold the bolt against it. Then slide the spring-loaded bolt back to expose the fixing points. You will need a little bit of clearance between the top of the bolt and the head of the frame, so that it does not catch when the door is used. If you intend to set in the receiver plate to finish flush with the frame face, use the thickness of the receiver plate to provide the clearance by placing it in between the end of the lock and the frame head. Hold the bolt in the required position and mark the screw positions with your bradawl (see Fig 6.24). When you have set in the receiver flush with the frame, you will have ample clearance for the door to close. If you don't intend to set the

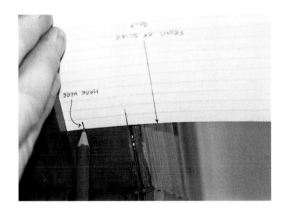

Fig 6.23 Use a card to determine the rear line of the receiver plate.

receiver plate into the frame you will need to allow a little more clearance than the receiver plate thickness. Two thicknesses of cardboard from the lock packaging plus the thickness of the receiver plate will be enough.

Fig 6.24 (right) Fitting a push bolt to the frame side of a door.

Fig 6.25 (below) The receiver plate in position.

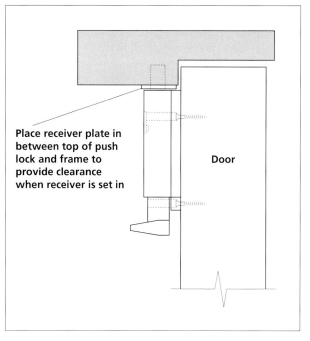

Place receiver plate in between top of push lock and frame to provide clearance when receiver is set in

Door

77

Once you have fitted the push bolt to the door, mark the centre of the receiver position by closing the door and pressing on the bolt. The bolt has a protruding centre point which will mark the frame for you, giving the centre point to drill out the bolt pocket. This done, hold the receiver plate over the mark, making sure it is parallel with the edge of the frame, and use a bradawl to mark the screw positions, after which you can fix the plate in position (see Fig 6.25).

Cross bolts

Cross bolts are tower bolts with the added security advantage of a flat cross bar which is slotted to allow it to drop over a padlock plate (see Fig 6.26). They are often used in more vulnerable positions (such as a rear garden gate) where access may be gained to the bolt. Always use a good quality padlock, and fit the bolt with single-direction security screws or cross-headed screws with the heads drilled out.

Fig 6.26 A cross bolt.

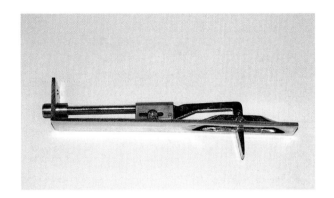

Fig 6.27 **A flush bolt.**

Flush bolts

Flush bolts are set into the door, flush with its surface, and are usually found on the leading edge of the static half of a pair of double doors (see Figs 6.27 and 6.28). The flush bolt requires the removal of a fair amount of wood to make room for its operating parts.

Fig 6.27 **A flush bolt.**

However, from a security point of view, you need to keep the amount of wood removed to a minimum, so careful marking out is important.

First measure the long face of the flush bolt, and transfer this figure to the chosen position on the door. The bolt should be fitted in the centre of the door edge, so if you measure the width of the stile and the width of the flush bolt all you need to do is take the measurement of the flush bolt away from the stile width and divide the remainder by two, giving the distance from the edge of the bolt to the edge of the door.

It is important to make sure the lock is *perfectly* vertical. Once you have worked out the distance from the door edge to the bolt, use a sharp pencil to mark the position of one edge of the bolt parallel with the door edge. Now hold the

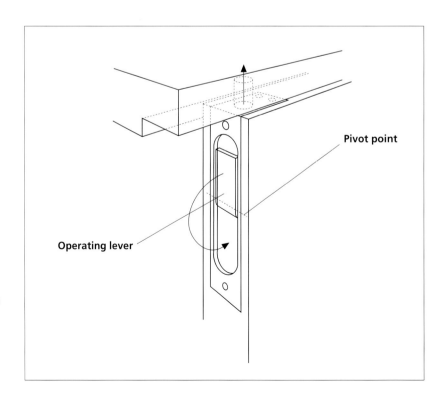

Pivot point

Operating lever

Fig 6.28 **Flush bolts are commonly found on sets of double doors, such as patio doors.**

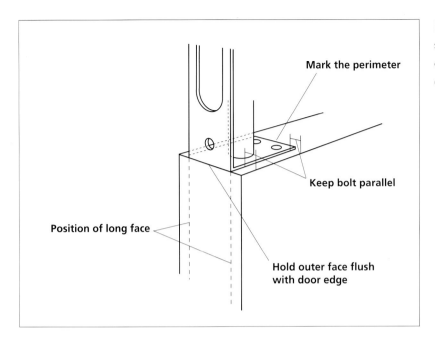

Fig 6.29 Mark the short face of the bolt onto the return face (top) of the door.

Mark the perimeter

Keep bolt parallel

Position of long face

Hold outer face flush with door edge

bolt against this mark, and mark the other side. You should now have two marks which run from the door corner to the mark indicating the length of the bolt. To mark the short face of the bolt, hold it in line with the two edge marks on the corner of the door, and flush with the door edge. Then mark the perimeter of the return face onto the door (see Fig 6.29).

Now assess how deep you need to cut to receive the various parts of the bolt. Lay the flush bolt on its side and measure the profile (see Fig 6.30). Remove the timber one level at a time and re-mark for the next level. First measure the thickness of the flush plate and carefully remove the whole area down to this level. There is a high risk of splitting the door edge when working so close to it, so support the edge of the door with side blocks held by clamps as shown in Fig 6.31.

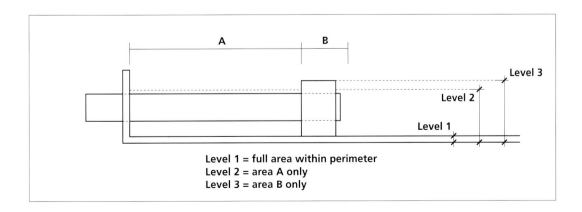

A   B

Level 3
Level 2
Level 1

Level 1 = full area within perimeter
Level 2 = area A only
Level 3 = area B only

Fig 6.30 Measure the profile of the bolt to establish the various depths of cut required to fit it in the door.

Fig 6.31 Support the door with blocks held by clamps while you cut the rebate to reduce the risk of splitting the edge.

Alternatively, you can run a tenon saw along the length of the perimeter line, which will separate the edge of the door from the area to be removed, reducing the risk of splitting the door edge when cutting the housing. Make sure you stay on the waste side of the line and don't cut too deep.

Work your chisel *along* the grain, starting at the centre of the area and carefully working towards the perimeter lines. Now mark out the areas which will need deepening to the next level, as shown in Fig 6.30 (areas A and B). Use a

Fig 6.32 Mark the frame with the bolt position.

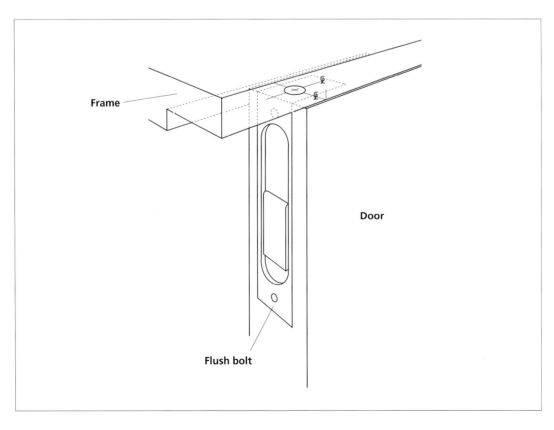

Frame

Door

Flush bolt

carpenters' brace to drill down to the next level and clean out the debris and square up the recesses with a sharp chisel. Now mark out the areas that need to be deepened to the next level and repeat the cutting and clearing process.

Once cutting is complete, try the flush bolt in the hole, and while it is in place try the lever mechanism for smooth operation before you fit the fixing screws; the action of the lever may need a little extra work to allow it to operate smoothly.

To mark out the receiver position for the flush bolt, close the door and mark the frame at the centre point of the door stile. Now open the door and operate the lock so that the slide bolt is in the locked position, close the door again so that the slide bolt touches the frame, and mark the centre of the bolt position on the frame. Now extend the two marks so that they cross each other, as shown in Fig 6.32. This is the centre point for the locking position. Measure the width of the slide bolt and select a drill bit as

close as possible to the bolt width while still allowing the bolt to operate effectively. Drill a hole deep enough to allow the lock to fully operate and fit the flat receiver plate in place centrally over the hole. If you wish to set in the receiver plate flush with the frame, mark round the perimeter of the plate with a sharp pencil and use a sharp chisel to carefully remove the timber to the required depth.

Vertical hoop and monkey-tail bolts

These are heavy-duty bolts, used on double doors, and have an extended tail to assist in their operation (see Fig 6.33). Like tower bolts, they are normally fitted flush with the bottom edge of the door, however, spring-loaded bolts are available

Fig 6.33 Vertical hoop (top) and monkey-tail (bottom) bolts.

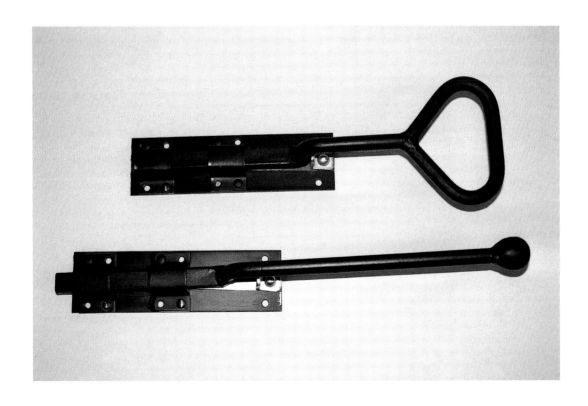

Fig 6.34 A spring-loaded chain bolt.

receiver box for these bolts, which is simply set into the floor in a mixture of sand and cement, mixed in proportions of one part cement and three parts sand, to finish level with the floor. Course grit sand is used in floor screed and concrete and would blend in better with an existing concrete floor than red building sand. If the floor area is of block paving take care not to allow the mixture of sand and cement to drop onto the driveway as the lime in the cement will stain the blocks and is very difficult to remove. If you are concerned about the driveway, cover the area with heavy gauge polythene or a large flattened cardboard box with a hole cut into it to work through before starting to set in the receiver box.

Spring-loaded chain bolts

These are a type of tower bolt designed for inaccessible locations, such as the top of very large doors. The chain is guided through a fixed hoop similar to the receiver on a standard tower bolt, and can be increased in length as required (see Fig 6.34). As with the standard tower bolt, the chain bolt is only effective as a security lock if access to operating the bolt is denied.

Foot bolts

These foot-operated bolts work by means of two levers, one at the top and a second on the front (see Fig 6.35). They are useful if you have your hands full or indeed have difficulty operating a standard slide bolt arrangement. Fitting a foot bolt involves the same process as fitting a tower bolt.

for use in a vertical, upper position. As these bolts are not supported with a lockable crossbar like the crossbolt in Fig 6.26, they should only be used in positions where access to operating the bolt is denied, inside a garage on the secondary door of a pair of double opening wooden doors which would complement the security locks fitted to the primary door. You are normally supplied with a

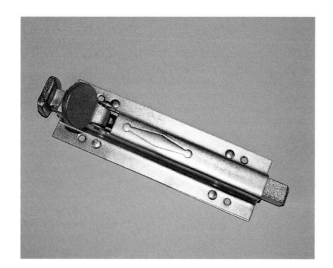

Fig 6.35 A foot bolt.

Door viewers and chains

7

Door viewers

A door viewer is a great asset to your security and safety. Purchase a viewer that provides a wide field of view, and give some thought to the lighting outside your door. There's no point in having a viewer if you cannot see who a night visitor is. If you have a porch light already, keep it switched on after dark, or consider fitting a sensor-activated light.

Fitting a door viewer

Viewers are easy to fit, but you must be very careful not to burst through the opposite face of the door when drilling the hole. The perimeter lip of a door viewer is very small and if you damage the door when fitting one it is unlikely to be masked by the viewer, and will also be at eye level and difficult to hide. There are three methods of fitting a viewer depending on the tools you have available.

Power drill and flat bit

If you have used a flat bit before you will know that it cuts at a higher speed than an auger bit. The level of vibration is also greater, so care is needed when making the cut. The power drill in this case need only be a standard tool and will not require variable speed or reverse action.

When cutting through a surface with two finished faces, such as a door, the cut should penetrate from both sides and meet in the middle. To do this you must be able to guarantee that the two cuts line up perfectly. You can remove the risk of bursting the door face *and* ensure that the two cuts line up, by gently drilling a small pilot hole through the door first, making sure you keep the drill level as you go. When the pilot hole is cut, isolate the drill and remove the small bit. Before fitting the flat bit into the drill, hold it against the door edge and wrap a piece of insulation tape around it at a point just beyond half the width of the door, to act as a depth gauge. As the main cut is at eye level and made at high speed you *must* use goggles to protect your eyes as you make the cut. Hold the power drill in position with the tip of the bit in the pilot hole and begin the cut, continuing up to the insulation tape, and then release the trigger of the drill allowing the drill to stop fully before pulling it out. This will reduce the risk of damaging the edge of the hole as you remove the bit from the cut. Once you have cut one side of the hole, position the tip of the flat bit into the pilot hole on the opposite face of the door and start making the final cut. When you enter the first cut there is a risk of pushing the flat bit completely through the door, so be very careful and find a balance between pushing the cut of the bit and not allowing it to run away with you when the cut is finished. If you do push the bit completely through the door, allow it to stop turning before pulling it back through the door; a flat bit has a tendency to jump about all over the place in this situation which could damage the door.

Power drill with hexagonal shank auger bit

Traditional self-drive auger bits can now be purchased with a hexagonal shank to fit into your power drill. Slow and steady are the words

to remember. To use this type of auger you need a power drill with variable speed to allow control over the cutting depth and reverse action so that the auger can be removed easily. A pilot hole is not needed as this would prevent the auger's self-drive thread from working. Hence, an alternative method is needed to ensure that the two cuts line up. Monitor the opposite face as you drill for signs of the auger point beginning to exit the face. Once the point of the auger can be seen, make the opposite cut. Remember to remove the auger as soon as you can see its tip. The threaded tip is designed to assist in pulling the auger into the wood. It does not actually make the cut; this is done by the cutting edge of the selected auger bit. If you continue to cut after the tip has emerged from the other side of the door, you will reduce the ability of the drive thread to pull the cut from the opposite side and will probably need to exert a little pressure to complete the cut.

The auger does not require high speed in order to do its job effectively, so do not operate your drill at high speed. Damage to the door could result.

Carpenters' brace and auger bit

A little more effort is needed to use a carpenters' brace (see Fig 7.1) but providing the auger is in good condition, very satisfactory results can be obtained. Remember that the drive thread is designed to pull the auger into the cut, so you need only turn the handle and keep the brace square to the door, rather than applying a great deal of pressure. Once again, you cannot drill a pilot hole as it would reduce the ability of the drive thread to pull the auger. Use the same method as that outlined above, regularly checking for the emerging auger tip. Once it begins to emerge, complete the cut from the opposite side of the door (see Fig 7.2).

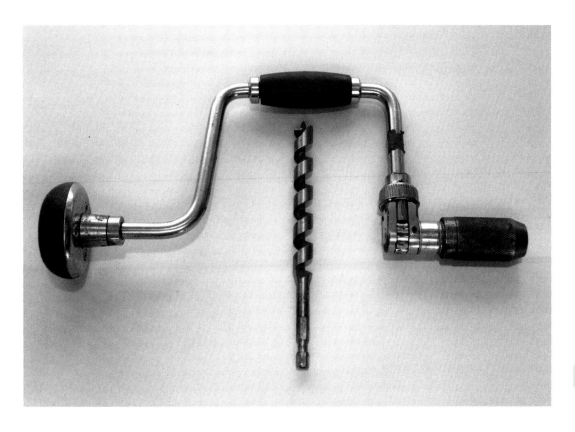

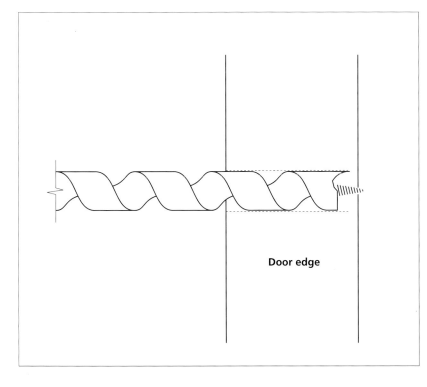

Door edge

Fig 7.1 (above) A carpenters' brace with a hexagonal shank auger bit.

Fig 7.2 (left) As soon as the tip of the auger begins to emerge from the other side of the door, stop drilling and begin again from the other side.

Once the hole is drilled, it is a very simple process to fit the viewer. One half of the unit has an internal thread, and the second half an external thread. If the viewer does not have a lens cover plate identifying the inner side, look through the viewer to confirm which half belongs on the inside. Separate the two halves of the unit and slide them through the door to meet in the middle. Then twist the two parts together to complete the job.

On a recent visit to a DIY stockist I spotted a viewer with a small viewing screen 50mm (2in) square, which would assist anyone who has

Fig 7.3 (above) A typical door chain, with a right-angled fixing plate (see also Fig 7.4).

Fig 7.4 (below) More secure chains have a right-angled fixing plate, affording greater resistance to forced entry.

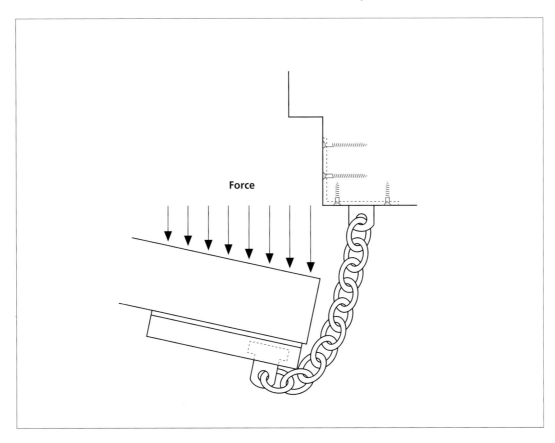

Force

difficulty getting close enough to a door to use a standard viewer comfortably. Such viewers require a larger hole in the door, but are well worth consideration.

Door chains

Never open a door before you have used the door viewer. If you are unsure of the visitor but feel the need to open the door, always use a door chain (see Fig 7.3).

Take a close look at the variety of chains available and try to purchase one which fixes into the side of the rebate and angles around the frame edge where the chain is fitted (see Fig 7.4). This reduces the risk of the screws being pulled out if the door is forced. You need to set in the door chain plate so that it is flush with the frame face and clears the door when it is in use, but this is well worth the effort for the added strength of the side fixing. If you can't get a side-fixing chain, improve the strength of a standard chain by upgrading the gauge (thickness) and length of the screws used to fit it to the frame. The more substantial types of chain have three screws holding the frame plate, with one of these set on a slight angle to the other two, which helps the unit grip the frame.

Drill pilot holes for the screws, to reduce the risk of splitting the frame.

8 Cylinder rim latches and bolts

Cylinder rim latches are surface-fixed units, so however much you pay for them, they will only be as strong as the screws that hold them in position. With this in mind, particular attention must be given to fitting the lock receiver box (sometimes known as the keep) and it is important that the frame to which it is fixed is sound, solid, and in good overall condition. The design of cylinder latches is such that the receiver box is not only fixed with screws to the inner face of the door frame (as in the case of the rim locks discussed in Chapter 10) but also wraps around the frame into the rebate, where it is fixed with two screws at 90° to the direction the door opens (see Fig 8.1). This fixing arrangement dramatically increases the holding power of the screws to resist forced entry, as the frame would need to be split apart in order to dislodge the receiver box.

There are a number of different types of cylinder latch on the market with a wide range of security and operational features, such as hacksaw resistance, automatic deadlocking, anti-twist cylinders, lock-picking resistant cylinders, and internal and external deadlocking. It is worth carefully considering the options available before spending your money.

Before you buy, remember to measure the width of your door stile to ensure that the lock will fit fully on the stile (see Fig 8.2). Also remember

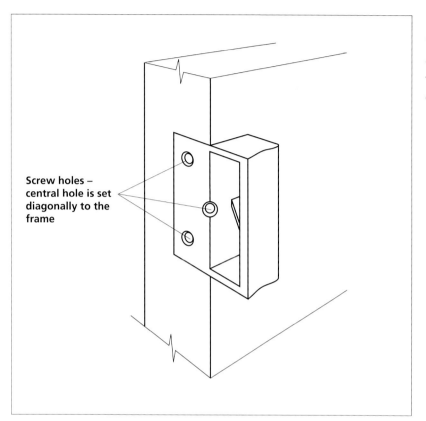

Screw holes – central hole is set diagonally to the frame

Fig 8.1 The receiver box should 'wrap around' the frame into the rebate, as here, for greater security.

Fig 8.2 Ensure that the lock will fit comfortably onto the stile.

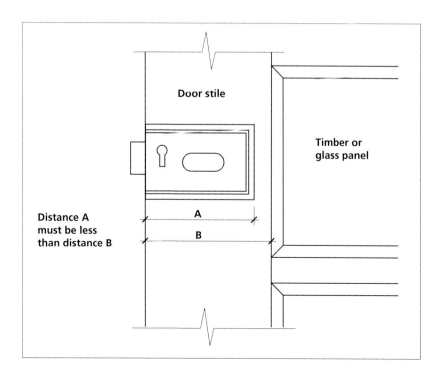

Door stile

Timber or glass panel

Distance A must be less than distance B

A

B

that any external door should have a good quality mortise deadlock fitted in addition to the cylinder lock. These are discussed in Chapter 5.

There are three main types of cylinder lock, and these are detailed below to assist you in making your choice.

Security rim latch with automatic external deadlocking

It is easy for an experienced burglar to open a tapered latch simply by inserting a plastic card between the door and the sill and sliding it down to push the latch open. If the door is glazed, it is even easier to break a pane of glass, reach in and operate the latch to gain entry. The same applies if the letter box has been positioned within reach of the latch and is large enough for a hand to be inserted. Automatic deadlocking provides security against both these means of entry. It is activated

as soon as the door is closed, so that the spring latch is locked in position. The lever action can also be locked in place with the key when you leave the property so that it cannot be operated by hand either. Remember that a deadlocked door cannot be opened from inside, so be sure you haven't locked anyone in.

Such locks improve the security of your house while you are out, but they cannot be deadlocked from the inside. If you want this facility you need to consider a security latch with internal deadlocking.

Security rim latch with automatic and internal deadlocking

These provide all the features of automatic deadlocks, with the additional feature of an internally-operated deadlock. Another advantage of these locks is that they can be operated from

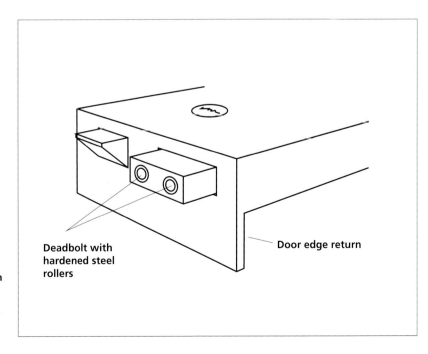

Deadbolt with hardened steel rollers

Door edge return

Fig 8.3 Deadbolt with hardened steel rollers to reduce the risk of being sawn through.

inside with the key provided, so you are in no danger of trapping someone inside accidentally as long as they know where the key is kept.

It is a common mistake to leave the key in the lock on the inside of the door when you retire for the night; this renders the door and you vulnerable to attack. Always remove the key.

Locks with internal and external deadbolts

These more substantial fittings are often recommended by police crime prevention officers, and offer a high level of security. They have a standard spring-loaded latch and a separate deadbolt, which, if used at all times, precludes any need for automatic deadlocking. The separate deadbolt has hardened steel rollers fitted (see Fig 8.3) to resist attack from sawing, and a double throw bolt. (The term double throw means that with two full turns of the key the bolt is thrown into the receiver to double the depth and therefore increase the lock's ability to withstand force.) These locks can be operated from inside or outside so you can secure the door at all times.

Fitting a cylinder rim latch lock

As cylinder latch units vary so greatly (the key hole position can range from 38mm (1½in) to 60mm (2⅜in) from the edge of the door), the following is a general guide only. Use it in conjunction with the instructions provided with your chosen lock and you should have no problems.

If the lock you are fitting has come from another door, and you have access to it, measure the distance from the edge of the door to the edge of the old cylinder hole. The cylinder hole usually measures 32mm (1¼in), but check the width just in case. If the hole is 32mm

(1¼in), add 16mm (⅝in) to the figure you got from the door edge to the edge of the hole and you have the distance to the centre of the cylinder on the new door. Very carefully cut the hole using a 32mm (1¼in) drill bit. Once the cut is made, slide the perimeter ring onto the cylinder and place the cylinder into the hole. You now need to fit the back plate on the opposite face of the door with the lugs outward and the flat latch operating bar poking through the centre hole. Hold the backplate in position and slide the two threaded bolts (three in the case of anti-twist cylinders) through the plate and into their respective positions in the rear of the cylinder unit. Tighten them finger-tight and gently nip them up with a screwdriver. Check the position of the cylinder to see if it needs straightening at all. Check that the backplate is set sufficiently back from the door edge to allow the face of the latch to finish flush with the door, and that it is parallel with the door edge. If you are happy with the position of the backplate, mark the two positions for the two fixing screws which hold it in place and fix the backplate to the door.

Position the body of the lock over the backplate. You may not be able to secure it just yet as some latches have a small extension of the latch face which needs to be set into the door edge (see Fig 8.3). If this is the case you will need to mark the perimeter of the door edge return and set it into the door. Now fix the lock body to the door. When you fit the receiver box, take care not to split the frame. Pilot the fixing points with a small drill bit before fitting the screws to reduce the chances of this happening.

Hold the receiver box over the latch, close the door and mark the upper and lower positions of the receiver onto the frame. Open the door again, line up the receiver against the two marks, and using a sharp pencil mark the perimeter of the door edge return where it enters the rebate (see Fig 8.4). Carefully remove the timber within the perimeter line so that the face of the plate finishes flush with the face of the rebate. You will notice that the three screws that hold the box in place are set as two at 90° to the frame and one on a diagonal into the frame (see Fig 8.1). At this stage fit only the single diagonal screw and try the latch operation. If you find it rattles when you close the door you may need to set the receiver into the frame on the front edge as well. Mark the perimeter of the box on the front face of the frame and remove just enough timber to stop the lock rattling. You will also need to extend the cut in the rebate to allow the box to set in further along the face of the rebate (see Fig 8.4). Return the receiver box to the frame and fix with the diagonal screw as before. Try the lock for smooth operation. When you are happy, pilot drill the positions for the two face screws, fix the receiver in position for the last time, and fit all the screws.

Upgrading an existing cylinder latch

If you have mislaid a set of keys or have recently moved into a new home, you may be concerned that others may hold a set of keys. It is possible to buy replacement cylinders for your existing rim latch, to save replacing the whole lock, but unfortunately you would still need to replace the additional mortise deadlocks on the door.

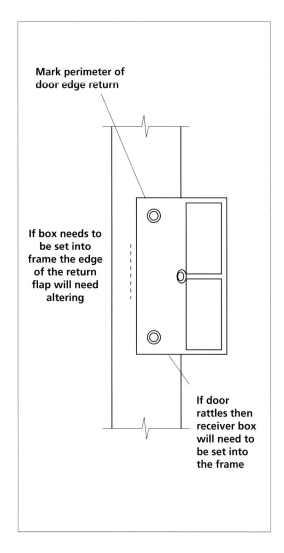

Fig 8.4 Positioning the cylinder latch receiver.

Hasps and staples

There is a wide variety of hasp and staple fittings on the market, suitable for a wide variety of applications and manufactured with a large range of finishes, including galvanized, chromium-plated, and plastic coated. The security of a hasp and staple unit is dependent on a number of important factors. The fixing screws must be concealed when it is locked, the opening being secured must be of sound construction, and the padlock used to secure the hasp must be of good quality. The wire hasp and staple (see Fig 9.1) is in common use but is not considered to be of significant value in terms of protecting your property. The screws are accessible and easy to remove, and the wire strap can easily be cut or forced open with a claw

Fig 9.1 **Wire hasp and staple.**

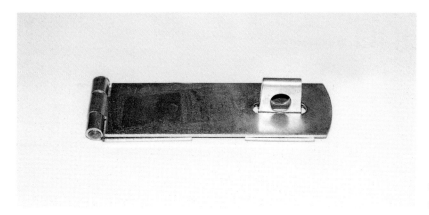

Fig 9.2 Medium-duty flat strap hasp and staple.

hammer. A better bet is the basic medium-duty flat strap hasp and staple (see Fig 9.2). These are inexpensive and available in a number of sizes. They have all their fixing screws concealed when the strap is in place, but they are constructed of a light gauge metal which could be twisted out of place with a strong bar. Their durability can be increased a little by using bolt fixings to fit the hasp and staple to the door and frame. When fitting the flat strap unit, it is important to make sure the two halves of the fitting line up correctly, by holding the assembled unit in position against the door and marking the outer edges of the strap. Fit the separate parts in their respective

places against the marks and fix either with screws or through-bolts, as appropriate.

A more substantial form of hasp and staple is the heavy-duty swivel type. These are strong, easy to fit and not too expensive (see Fig 9.3). All the fixing screws are concealed when secured; they are made from a heavy gauge metal and can be bolted through the door. Make sure the vertical pin of the latch receiver plate intended for the frame is strong enough to withstand a sideways bashing or leverage. Bending this pin sideways could release the still-locked, heavy duty horizontal strap and allow the door to open. Keep this in mind when you decide what to store in the area protected by the lock.

94

Fig 9.3 Heavy-duty swivel hasp and staple.

As you move up the price range a little, you will find a number of compact, heavy duty, solid and more secure fittings. Sometimes they are called padbars and again, they are only as good as the strength of the mounting point they are fixed to. They are available in straight flat bar or middle hinge cranked (see Fig 9.4) for internal frame fitting. It is recommended that they are fitted using through-bolts for added security.

Padlocks

A good quality padlock will only be effective if the hasp and staple is fitted correctly to a sound structure. If an expensive padlock is fitted to an inferior fitting you have wasted your money, and will probably lose the padlock as well as the items in the outhouse!

The ability of a good quality padlock to be an effective deterrent is dependent upon two things: the locking mechanism within, and the quality of the shackle. Padlocks also vary in that some have long, exposed shackles which are very easy to lever open, strike with a blow to

Fig 9.4 **Hasp and staple with cranked middle hinge.**

release the lock or cut with a hacksaw or bolt cutters. These are known as open-shackle padlocks. More secure types of padlock have shortened, hardened steel shackles which are also protected by the extended body of the padlock, providing additional protective cover. These are called closed-shackle padlocks, and are highly recommended.

95

10 Rim locks

R im locks (or surface locks) are surface-fixed to the door, and the body of the lock held in position by three or four fixing screws. You can buy these locks in a variety of finishes: chrome, brass or painted black, but they all have the same characteristics.

The standard rim lock (see Fig 10.1) can only be considered to be as strong as the two screws holding the receiver in place and can be purchased with both latch and bolt for general use or dead bolt only.

Rim locks are often found on garden gates, rear entrance doors and especially internal doors of the panelled Victorian style. They are not normally found on main entrance doors. I have

Fig 10.1 A standard rim lock.

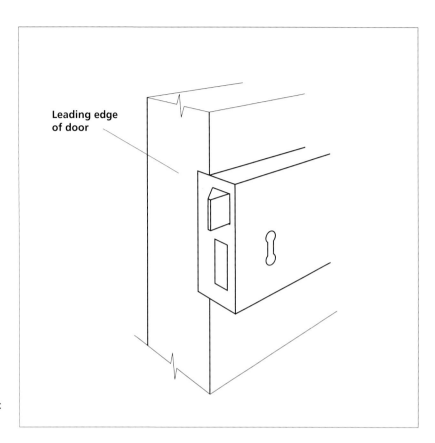

**Leading edge
of door**

Fig 10.2 **Hold the
end plate hard against
the edge of the door.**

mentioned a number of times that surface fixing locks are more vulnerable than mortise locks, because the screws are fixed in the same direction as any force put upon them if entry is attempted. The receiver box used with rim locks is normally not very heavy and could buckle if forced, therefore the lock should be supported by an additional security device to back it up. If the location under consideration is a back gate or door, you may consider a tower bolt as described in Chapter 6. If the door is internal, consider using dead bolts as described in Chapter 3, and hinge upgrading as described in Chapter 4. If you feel that a rim lock suits your requirements, it is very simple to fit, but you need to be precise with the side cuts for the door knob and escutcheon plate (key plate). The size of the escutcheon plate doesn't make any allowances for widening out

the hole if it is not in line when the lock is fitted, so take it slowly. If the fixing screws enter the key hole you may need to use adhesive to fix the plate rather than the screws.

Fitting a rim lock to a solid timber door

Hold the rim lock against the door stile in the chosen position with the small end plate hard against the leading edge of the door (see Fig 10.2). If the lock is in a position where the finish is important you may choose to set the small extended end plate in, flush with the door edge. If it is not important to the finished job you don't have to do this as long as the lock will not catch on the frame when you close the door. If you decide to set in the end plate, do so prior to

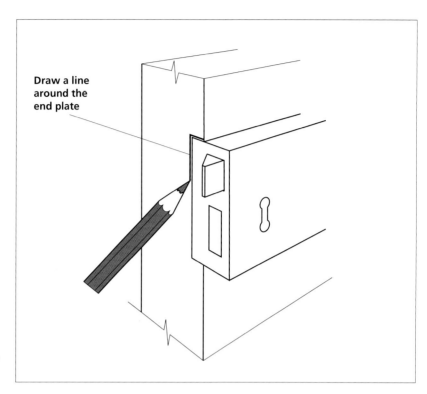

Fig 10.3 Mark the position of the extended end plate for setting in.

Fig 10.4 Typical door furniture for a rim lock.

marking the positions for the door furniture as setting in the return end will alter the position slightly. If you decide to set it flush with the door, hold the lock in the chosen position and draw around the extended end plate with a sharp pencil (see Fig 10.3). Notice that the return plate may not be very thick so take care not to remove too much timber; it only needs to be flush with the surface. You are now ready to mark the spindle and key positions onto the door face.

To determine the spindle position the lock must be held in its intended place. Place a

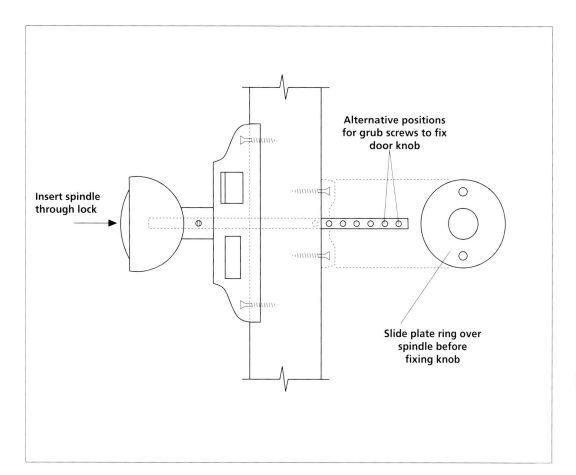

Alternative positions for grub screws to fix door knob

Insert spindle through lock

Slide plate ring over spindle before fixing knob

99

Fig 10.5 Fitting the spindle and knob furniture.

bradawl through the body of the lock and mark the centre of the spindle position. Use a 16mm (⅝in) auger to cut the spindle position, taking care not to burst through the opposite face of the door. Either clamp a block to the opposite face of the door and drill into it, or cut the position from both sides of the door when the exit point is evident by the auger tip breaking through the door face.

To determine the key hole position, place the bradawl through the lock and mark the door at both the upper and lower ends of the slot. The upper mark will provide the centre point for a 9mm (⅜in) auger and allow clearance for the key to pass through the door into the lock. The lower mark will give you the extreme end of the slot. If you cut beyond this mark your cut may not be covered by the small escutcheon plate on the opposite side of the door. Using a 6mm (¼in) chisel, work away from the 9mm (⅜in) hole in small cuts towards the lower mark.

With the furniture and key access points cut, you can now hold the lock body in position and fix it in place with the screws provided. The operating knob (see Figs 10.4 and 10.5) is held onto the spindle with a small grub screw, and once the knob and spindle have been put together you can slide the spindle through the rim lock into the door, until it is fully against the lock (see Fig 10.5).

Fig 10.6 Adjust the position of the receiver box to reduce free movement of the door when closed.

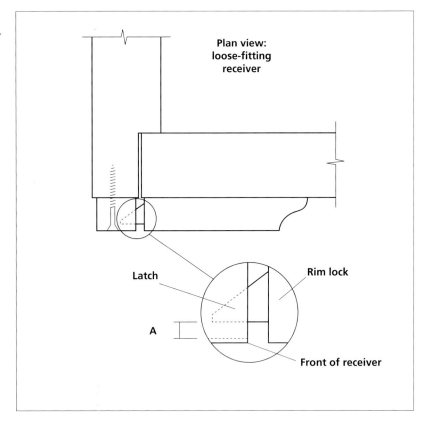

Plan view: loose-fitting receiver

Latch

Rim lock

A

Front of receiver

You will now be able to see the spindle sticking out of the door on the opposite side, and will notice a series of threaded holes along its length. These provide alternative positions for the second grub screw if you need to reduce the length of the spindle to suit the thickness of the door (see Fig 10.5). Slide the ring plate over the spindle, and then slide the second knob into position to touch the ring plate. If all the components fit together then the spindle is of a suitable length and you can fit the second grub screw. If you find that the spindle is still visible then measure the distance between the parts held apart and reduce the spindle by that amount, after which you can fit the second grub screw.

Fitting the receiver of a rim lock is very simple. Close the door and hold the receiver box

in position over the latch, in line with the body of the lock. Use a bradawl to break the wood grain and pilot a hole for the two fixing screws. Fit the screws through the receiver box into the frame. Close the door to check the operation of the lock. If the door still moves back and forth when it is closed, you will need to set the receiver box into the frame. Measure the distance from the flat face of the latch to the inner face of the receiver (distance A in Fig 10.6). Use a sharp pencil to mark the perimeter of the receiver box. Remove the receiver box and mark the required depth of the cut onto the door frame.

Carefully remove the timber within the perimeter line down to the marked depth where the flat face of the latch is in line with the inner edge of the receiver box.

Electrical and electronic accessories

Outside the home

Infra-red sensor units will detect both body heat and movement from a good distance and activate high intensity lights to flood the entire area. When purchasing this type of unit, be sure that the spread of light given off is sufficient for the area. It is also very important when positioning the unit that you consider carefully any areas that may be placed in heavy, 'artificial' shadow such as bushes, the corners of outhouses and so on, allowing an intruder to hop from point to point up to the house, hiding in these shadows without being spotted. The infra-red unit should also detect any movement against the perimeter wall of the house to ensure that if an intruder runs the whole length of the garden to seek shelter beneath the sensor, they won't find any.

With regard to the shadowed areas, you would be advised to consider possible ways of reducing the effect. With a bush you may think about thinning it out, allowing light to pass right through it. Corners of outhouses are a little more difficult but you can fit an extension light to the infra-red system. You might also consider the possibility of fitting an angled mirror adjacent to the extension light so you can see around the corner without leaving the house and be assured of your safety.

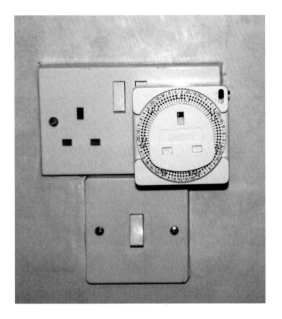

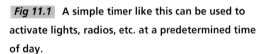

Fig 11.1 A simple timer like this can be used to activate lights, radios, etc. at a predetermined time of day.

Fig 11.2 A programmable security lampholder.

Inside the home

There are many units available that simply plug into the mains which will operate table lamps, standard lamps or radios at the time set on the programmer. Many can be programmed over a 24-hour or 7-day period, and also have random activating facilities.

More basic units are set by turning a programming disc as seen in Fig 11.1, allowing for 24-hour programming.

If you feel it would be more beneficial to have the main house lights operating instead of lamps then there are alternatives to consider.

A security light switch looks and operates as a normal light switch, and is designed to replace it. It allows you to programme when the main light goes on and off. *Do not* attempt the switch replacement unless you are a qualified electrician: electricity can kill.

If you do not wish to change the light switch fittings but would still prefer the main lights to come on automatically, you can fit a programmable security lampholder into an existing light fitting, just like a lightbulb but in between the lightbulb and the bulbholder (see Fig 11.2). The unit can also be used in table lamps or standard lamps, but you must make sure that they are in a good position to get as much natural light as possible for the light sensor unit to operate effectively. They are available as dawn-to-dusk activated units, or as programmable units, and some have the option of intermittent timers which will activate at various times throughout the night. The fitting also allows you to reposition the light shade onto the auto sensor in the normal fashion.

Consider fitting a key-operated door security alarm (see Fig 11.3). These are battery-operated, and have two optional settings; an immediate response alarm, or an exit and entry time delay

Fig 11.3 (right) A key-operated door security alarm.

setting, which is simple to set. The alarm is fixed to the door either by screws, in which case you are supplied with a paper template for accurate positioning, or by means of a large, double-sided adhesive pad, also supplied with the alarm.

You can also buy code-operated alarms (see Fig 11.4), which have all the benefits of a key-operated alarm and are fitted in the same way but provide an additional setting in the form of a visitor entry beep each time the door is opened. You have 1,680 choices of code combinations to choose from to set and deactivate the alarm, and it has a small light on the face to warn that it is activated. Sometimes a warning light is all it takes to deter an intruder.

Finally, another alternative is an internal door alarm. These are very simple to set (see Fig 11.5); just switch on or off by means of the small top switch and you're in business. While sold as door alarms, these can also be used on windows.

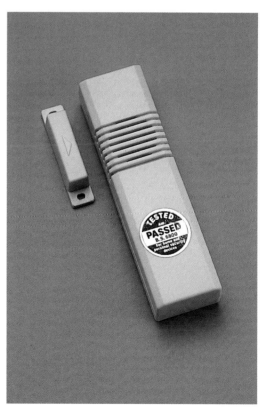

Fig 11.4 (below) A code-operated alarm.

Fig 11.5 (above) An internal door alarm.

Glossary

auger wood-cutting bit used in a carpenters' brace or electric power drill.

bevel an edge which is at any angle other than a right angle; also refers to the grinding and sharpening angles of wood chisels.

bradawl hand-pressed, metal, square-edged blade fitted to a hardwood handle, used to pilot holes to take screws, thereby reducing the risk of timber splitting.

chamfer an angle planed at an edge.

circlip small circular clip designed to hold lock levers in place.

cockspur lever handle for securing side-hung sash windows.

cylinder component of a cylinder rim lock which provides key operation from the outside of the property.

deadbolt small, key-operated bolt used at the top and bottom of a door or opening sash.

deadlock substantial five-lever mortise lock fitted in addition to the general operational locks on an external door.

dowels cylindrical lengths of timber used in the construction of modern doors.

drive thread thread found on the tip of a wood cutting auger bit providing pull for the cutting action.

escutcheon key hole cover plate used on deadlocks and bolts.

faceplate visible face of a mortise lock.

flat bit wood-cutting bit for use in a power drill.

furniture door ironmongery such as handles, knobs, letterplates, escutcheons, etc.

galvanization treatment of metal components against the effect of weather deterioration.

grain the arrangement and direction of the wood fibres.

grub screw small, square-ended screw designed to fit into a threaded component.

hanging stile the side of a door frame to which the hinges are attached.

haunch a short projection at the side of a tenon, designed to resist any twisting tendency.

hinge bound a door with an incorrectly positioned hinge which causes the door to spring open.

hinge leaf the flat, plate section of a hinge.

house-in removal of timber in order to sink a component so that it is flush with the surface.

intumescent strip fire restriction strip fitted to the rebate of a door frame or a door's leading edge.

infra-red sensor heat detection sensor to pick up body movement.

jamb vertical side of a window frame.

knuckle locking section of a hinge.

latch spring-loaded catch operated by a door handle.

leading edge narrow edge of a door into which a mortise lock is fitted.

lever handles ironmongery used to operate a latch.

lipping narrow strip of timber fitted to the leading edge of a flush door.

locking stile vertical edge of a door which is home to the latch, locks and furniture.

meeting rail adjoining horizontal rail of the upper and lower frames of a vertical sliding sash window.

mortise hole cut to receive a tenon.

mullion vertical middle member of a window frame.

offer up hold in the intended position.

pare off the smoothing of irregularities in the surface of wood. Usually performed with a broad chisel.

pilot hole pre-drilled guide hole for a screw.

proud protruding above the surface.

rails horizontal members of a door.

rawl plug purpose-made sleeve used to grip the inner surface of a drilled hole to give purchase for a screw.

rebate stepped edge of a frame used to house glass in windows or for a door to close into.

receiver plate metal plate fitted to receive latches, bolts and locks.

rim lock lock designed to fit to the surface edge of a door.

self tap screws which are designed to cut their own thread in aluminium windows.

sill timber section in a window frame, grooved to take the internal window board and extended externally to provide a weather drip.

spindle square-sectioned bar which connects one side of the door furniture to the other, passing through the lock.

stay arm used to hold an opening sash window in the desired position.

stiles vertical timber sides of a door or window.

tenon timber joint cut to house into a mortise.

transom horizontal member of a window frame separating the lower glazed panel from the upper opening sash.

window board inner flat board required to span the thickness of the wall from the window frame to the inside of the house.

Tools for the task

The following list shows how few tools are actually needed in order to fit security items. If you have not already got these basic tools at home, they are easily acquired without great expense.

Auger bits

These are available for use in a carpenters' brace only (with a square shank), or for use in both a brace and an electric drill. Do not try to use these bits in an electric drill unless it has variable speed for a slow delivery of power and reverse action so that you can remove it from the hole when the required depth has been reached. If you want the auger to stop cutting, let go of the trigger: remember who is in charge!

Bradawl

Make sure the bradawl you use has a flat, chisel-point end, not a pointed spike. A pointed spike will separate the grain of the wood, causing it to split along the grain when you insert a screw into the pilot hole. A chisel point inserted at 90° to the grain will break the grain and greatly reduce the risk of the wood splitting.

Carpenters' brace

This is needed for the larger items, where a deep mortise is needed to house a lock or to provide key and door furniture access at the side of the door. Auger cutting bits with a worm thread (rather than flat bits) to pull the cutting edge are used in this time-honoured tool.

Chisel

Chisels can be rather expensive, but always buy the best you can afford. Good quality chisels will give you excellent service over many years if you keep them sharp. If you are not familiar with the method for sharpening chisels, a small tool called a 'honing guide' (available from DIY tool stockists) will give you all the help you need. When using a chisel, never try to remove too much timber in one go: 'more haste, less speed' is the rule to bear in mind.

Combination square

This is basically a steel rule with a sliding fence set at 90° to it. It is possible to fit locks and other devices without a combination square, but it is a very useful tool for assessing parallel and centre lines.

Flat bits

These are for use in a power drill and are relatively inexpensive. They operate at high speed and do not have a worm thread like the auger bits, so can be removed easily. A basic electric drill is required: reverse action is not necessary, but you might find it easier to use if the drill has variable speed, although this is not essential. Always use eye protection as the drill bits throw out a lot of debris during cutting.

Insulation tape

Use insulation tape to wrap around the cutting bits to act as a depth guide when drilling.

Mallet

A wooden or rubber mallet is needed to work a chisel. Do not be tempted to use the side of a hammer instead, as it will damage the top of the chisel.

Marking gauge

The most basic type of gauge is a single pin set into an arm with a sliding square stock which can be locked at any point along its length. Other types of gauge are also available, such as the mortise gauge, which has a single pin on one face of the arm and a pair of pins on the opposite face that are independently adjustable, or the cutting gauge, which has a flat, sharp-edged pin that can cut across the grain when required.

Screwdrivers

There is a wide choice of screwdrivers on the market and a huge variation in quality. Generally speaking, cheap screwdrivers are uncomfortable to use and the working edge can twist off easily with very little resistance. As with the chisels, try to buy the best you can afford: you will be rewarded in terms of comfort and strength.

Steel tape

This is useful for positioning items correctly before fitting.

Useful addresses

Chubb Locks Ltd
PO Box 197
Wednesfield Road
Wolverhampton
WV10 0ET
Tel: 01902 455111

N T Legge Ltd
Moat Street
Willenhall
West Midlands
WV13 1TD
Tel: 01902 707494

Polycell Products Ltd
Broadwater Road
Welwyn Garden City
Herts
AL7 3AZ
Tel: 01707 328131

Yale Security Products Ltd
Wood Street
Willenhall
West Midlands
WV13 1LA
Tel: 01902 366911

Metric conversion table

inches to millimetres and centimetres
mm = millimetres cm = centimetres

inches	mm	cm	inches	cm	inches	cm
⅛	3	0.3	9	22.9	30	76.2
¼	6	0.6	10	25.4	31	78.7
⅜	10	1.0	11	27.9	32	81.3
½	13	1.3	12	30.5	33	83.8
⅝	16	1.6	13	33.0	34	86.4
¾	19	1.9	14	35.6	35	88.9
⅞	22	2.2	15	38.1	36	91.4
1	25	2.5	16	40.6	37	94.0
1¼	32	3.2	17	43.2	38	96.5
1½	38	3.8	18	45.7	39	99.1
1¾	44	4.4	19	48.3	40	101.6
2	51	5.1	20	50.8	41	104.1
2½	64	6.4	21	53.3	42	106.7
3	76	7.6	22	55.9	43	109.2
3½	89	8.9	23	58.4	44	111.8
4	102	10.2	24	61.0	45	114.3
4½	114	11.4	25	63.5	46	116.8
5	127	12.7	26	66.0	47	119.4
6	152	15.2	27	68.6	48	121.9
7	178	17.8	28	71.1	49	124.5
8	203	20.3	29	73.7	50	127.0

Index

WOODWORKING

40 More Woodworking Plans & Projects	GMC Publications
Bird Boxes and Feeders for the Garden	Dave Mackenzie
Complete Woodfinishing	Ian Hosker
Electric Woodwork	Jeremy Broun
Furniture Projects	Rod Wales
Furniture Restoration (Practical Crafts)	Kevin Jan Bonner
Furniture Restoration for Beginners	Kevin Jan Bonner
Green Woodwork	Barry Jackson
Incredible Router	Jeremy Broun
Making & Modifying Woodworking Tools	Jim Kingshott
Making Chairs and Tables	GMC Publications
Making Fine Furniture	Tom Darby
Making Little Boxes from Wood	John Bennett
Making Shaker Furniture	Barry Jackson
Making Unusual Miniatures	Graham Spalding
Pine Furniture Projects	Dave Mackenzie
Security for the Householder:	
Fitting locks and other devices	E. Phillips
Sharpening Pocket Reference Book	Jim Kingshott
Sharpening: The Complete Guide	Jim Kingshott
Tool Making for Woodworkers	Ray Larsen
Woodfinishing Handbook (Practical Crafts)	Ian Hosker
Woodworking Plans/Projects	GMC Publications
The Workshop	Jim Kingshott

WOODTURNING

Adventures in Woodturning	David Springett
Bert Marsh: Woodturner	Bert Marsh
Bill Jones' Notes from the Turning Shop	Bill Jones
Bill Jones' Further Notes from the Turning Shop	Bill Jones
Colouring Techniques for Woodturners	Jan Sanders
Decorative Techniques for Woodturners	Hilary Bowen
Essential Tips for Woodturners	GMC Publications
Faceplate Turning	GMC Publications
Fun at the Lathe	R.C. Bell
Illustrated Woodturning Techniques	John Hunnex
Keith Rowley's Woodturning Projects	Keith Rowley
Make Money from Woodturning	Ann & Bob Phillips
Multi-Centre Woodturning	Ray Hopper
Pleasure and Profit from Woodturning	Reg Sherwin
Practical Tips for Turners & Carvers	GMC Publications
Practical Tips for Woodturners	GMC Publications
Spindle Turning	GMC Publications
Turning Miniatures in Wood	John Sainsbury
Turning Wooden Toys	Terry Lawrence
Understanding Woodturning	Ann & Bob Phillips
Useful Woodturning Projects	GMC Publications
Woodturning: A Foundation Course	Keith Rowley
Woodturning Jewellery	Hilary Bowen
Woodturning Masterclass	Tony Boase
Woodturning: A Sourcebook Of Shapes	John Hunnex
Woodturning Techniques	GMC Publications
Woodturning Wizardry	David Springett

WOODCARVING

The Art of the Woodcarver	GMC Publications
Carving Birds & Beasts	GMC Publications
Carving on Turning	GMC Publications
Carving Realistic Birds	David Tippey
Decorative Woodcarving	Jeremy Williams
Essential Tips for Woodcarvers	GMC Publications
Essential Woodcarving Techniques	Dick Onians
Lettercarving in Wood	Chris Pye
Understanding Woodcarving	GMC Publications
Wildfowl Carving - Volume 1	Jim Pearce
Wildfowl Carving - Volume 2	Jim Pearce
The Woodcarvers	GMC Publications
Woodcarving: A Complete Course	Ron Butterfield
Woodcarving for Beginners	GMC Publications
Woodcarving: A Foundation Course	Zoë Gertner
Woodcarving Tools, Materials & Equipment	Chris Pye

UPHOLSTERY

Seat Weaving (Practical Crafts)	Ricky Holdstock
Upholsterer's Pocket Reference Book	David James
Upholstery: A Complete Course	David James
Upholstery Restoration Projects	David James
Upholstery Techniques & Projects	David James

TOYMAKING

Designing & Making Wooden Toys	*Terry Kelly*	Making Wooden Toys & Games	*Jeff & Jennie Loader*
Fun to Make Wooden Toys and Games	*Jeff & Jennie Loader*	Restoring Rocking Horses	*Clive Green & Anthony Dew*
Making Board Peg & Dice Games	*Jeff & Jennie Loader*		

DOLLS' HOUSES

Architecture for Dolls' Houses	*Joyce Percival*	Making Georgian Dolls' Houses	*Derek & Sheila Rowbottom*
Beginners' Guide to the Dolls' House Hobby	*Jean Nisbett*	Making Period Dolls' House Accessories	*Andrea Barham*
The Complete Dolls' House Book	*Jean Nisbett*	Making Period Dolls' House Furniture	*Derek & Sheila Rowbottom*
Dolls' House Bathrooms - Lots of Little Loos	*Patricia King*	Making Tudor Dolls' Houses	*Derek & Sheila Rowbottom*
Easy to Make Dolls' House Accessories	*Andrea Barham*	Making Victorian Dolls' House Furniture	*Patricia King*
Make Your Own Dolls' House Furniture	*Maurice Harper*	Miniature Needlepoint Carpets	*Janet Granger*
Making Dolls' House Furniture	*Patricia King*	The Secrets of the Dolls' House Makers	*Jean Nisbett*

CRAFTS

Celtic Knotwork Designs	*Sheila Sturrock*	Embroidery Tips & Hints	*Harold Hayes*
Collage from Seeds, Leaves and Flowers	*Joan Carver*	Introduction to Pyrography (Practical Crafts)	*Stephen Poole*
Complete Pyrography	*Stephen Poole*	Making Knitwear Fit	*Pat Ashforth & Steve Plummer*
Creating Knitwear Designs	*Pat Ashforth & Steve Plummer*	Tassel Making for Beginners	*Enid Taylor*
Cross Stitch Kitchen Projects	*Janet Granger*	Tatting Collage	*Lindsay Rogers*
Cross Stitch on Colour	*Sheena Rogers*		

VIDEOS

Drop-in and Pinstuffed Seats	*David James*	Classic Profiles	*Dennis White*
Stuffover Upholstery	*David James*	Twists and Advanced Turning	*Dennis White*
Elliptical Turning	*David Springett*	Sharpening the Professional Way	*Jim Kingshott*
Woodturning Wizardry	*David Springett*	Sharpening Turning & Carving Tools	*Jim Kingshott*
Turning Between Centres	*Dennis White*	Bowl Turning	*John Jordan*
Turning Bowls	*Dennis White*	Hollow Turning	*John Jordan*
Boxes, Goblets & Screw Threads	*Dennis White*	Woodturning: A Foundation Course	*Keith Rowley*
Novelties and Projects	*Dennis White*	Carving a Figure - The Female Form	*Ray Gonzalez*

MAGAZINES

WOODTURNING · WOODCARVING · TOYMAKING

FURNITURE & CABINETMAKING · BUSINESSMATTERS

CREATIVE IDEAS FOR THE HOME · THE ROUTER

The above represents a full list of all titles currently published or scheduled to be published. All are available direct from the Publishers or through bookshops, newsagents and specialist retailers.

To place an order, or to obtain a complete catalogue, contact:

GMC Publications,
166 High Street, Lewes, East Sussex BN7 1XU United Kingdom
Tel: 01273 488005 Fax: 01273 478606

Orders by credit card are accepted